The
JEWS
in the time of
JESUS
A History

Peter Connolly

Oxford University Press

Oxford University Press, Walton Street, Oxford OX2 6DP

Oxford New York Toronto
Delhi Bombay Calcutta Madras Karachi
Kuala Lumpur Singapore Hong Kong Tokyo
Nairobi Dar es Salaam Cape Town
Melbourne Auckland Madrid

and associate companies in
Berlin Ibadan

Oxford is a trade mark of Oxford University Press

First published in hardback as
Living in the Time of Jesus of Nazareth 1983
Reprint 1988, 1991, 1992, 1993
First published in paperback 1994

ISBN 0 19 910162 0

The author would like to thank the following: Dr. Doron
Mendels of the Hebrew University at Jerusalem and the
Reverend Richard Hughes for reading and checking the text.
Also, Michal Dayaggi Mendels of the Israel Museum for her
help and encouragement.

The author and publishers would like to thank the following
for permission to reproduce photographs: David Alexander,
p. 36; Zev Radovan, p. 15; Alan Hutchison Library/Bernard
Régent, pp. 82/3 (bottom). All other photographs are
copyright of the author.

Phototypeset by Tradespools Ltd., Frome, Somerset
Printed in Hong Kong

Contents

1

HEROD THE GREAT

Flight to Masada

The hubbub died down, the lights faded and darkness descended on the city. Silently the gates were pushed open and a long column of fugitives slipped down into the valley. They headed south across the hills towards Bethlehem. From their rich apparel and the large retinue of soldiers and servants it was clear that these were no ordinary refugees. Their leader was a powerfully built man in his early thirties. He looked furtively over his shoulder as if he expected any minute to see pursuing horsemen on the sky-line and to hear their arrows whispering throught the night air. Among the fugitives were his mother, his sister and his bride-to-be, the beautiful Miriam. The women and children, tears streaming down their faces, turned their backs on their beloved Jerusalem – perhaps for ever. His mother was too old to sit on a donkey and she travelled in a cart. As they stumbled through the darkness the wheel of the cart hit an obstruction and overturned, throwing the old lady to the ground. At first he thought that she was dead and his heart sank. But he managed to revive her and the column continued on its way.

By day-break they had passed Bethlehem. A few marauding Parthians attacked but were driven off. Next they were surprised by a band of Jewish rebels but once more managed to fight their way through. When the group reached Idumaea their leader felt a little more secure, for this was his native land. He held a council of war.

It was agreed that his closest family, guarded by the light armed troops, about 800 in all, should take refuge in the precipitous fortress of Masada which towered above the western shore of the Dead Sea. Masada had sufficient supplies of grain and water to withstand a prolonged siege. The rest of his followers were ordered to disperse.

Having taken his family to safety on the rocky citadel and repaired its walls, the young man set off southwards. The Arabs refused him sanctuary so he rode on towards Egypt and at Alexandria he was welcomed by the exotic Cleopatra who was about three years his junior. The young queen received him with honour and arranged for him to be taken by sea to Rome. Over the next few years they were to become the bitterest of enemies. But Cleopatra can hardly have realized that here was the future king of the Jews – Herod the Great.

Herod inspecting the newly completed south-western entrance to the temple precinct. The temple which was begun in 20/19BC took some 60 years to complete. It was the greatest of Herod's many building projects. Even today the vast artificial platform on which the temple was built dominates Jerusalem.

Herod and his party are at the top of the steps. His Gallic bodyguard keep him isolated from the population who hated him because he was not a full blooded Jew.

Since 1967 this whole area has been excavated so that we now have a fairly accurate idea of what the original building looked like.

A Land of Strife

As Herod sailed for Rome he must have often thought back over the events that had led to his flight from Jerusalem. Nearly 300 years before Alexander the Great had conquered the vast Persian empire of which Jerusalem had been a part. After Alexander's death his generals divided up the empire between them. The eastern end of the Mediterranean became the kingdoms of Egypt and Syria. Judea, the home of the Jews, belonged to Egypt but was claimed by Syria.

More than a century before Herod's birth, Judea had come under the control of Syria. A generation later the King of Syria, Antiochus IV, decided to reorganise his realm to give it the benefits of Greek civilization and thought. He decided to bring these same advantages to the Jews. When he insisted that they change their religious practices to more fashion-

able Greek forms a revolt broke out. It was led by the Maccabaean brothers. The Syrians tried to put down the rebellion but failed. So Judea became virtually independent, and was ruled by the Maccabaean family, the Hasmonaeans. They became the high priests and the governors of the country. To keep Syria in check the Hasmonaeans made treaties with Rome, the new super-power in the west.

Over the next half-century the tiny Judean state gradually grew in strength, and conquered the surrounding lands. In the north Samaria and Galilee were captured. In the south and east the Idumaeans and Peraeans were overcome and forced to adopt the Jewish religion. Herod was an Idumaean. It was during this period that the Jewish religion split into two opposing groups – the Pharisees and Sadducees.

The Judaean kingdom

During the period dealt with in this book Palestine was divided into seven main areas. West of the Jordan valley were Galilee, Samaria, Judaea and Idumaea whilst to the east were Gaulantis (modern Golan), the Decapolis (the ten cities), and Peraea. These were the most important provinces. There were other lesser areas which will be dealt with in passing. Besides these there was also Phoenicia in the north-west which was part of the Roman province of Syria and the coastal strip which Pompey took under Roman control.

BELOW: southern Idumaea which verges on the desert. It is the home of the wandering Bedouin tribesmen. Their typical tents and flocks of goats can be seen in this picture. In ancient times the area provided a harvest of barley and was used as grazing land for sheep. Northern Idumaea is very similar to Judea and Samaria.

Plains and hills

Palestine is a predominantly hilly country but there is an extensive plain along the coast stretching from Mount Carmel in the north to the desert in the south. Another smaller marshy plain stretches south east along the north side of the Carmel ridge. This is known as the Plain of Esdraelon or the valley of Jezreel. The valley of the Jordan is also often referred to as a plain.

The great depression

The Jordan valley is an extension of the great Rift Valley which stretches for some 6,500 kilometres up through East Africa and the Red Sea. Many millions of years ago this area of Israel formed part of the Red Sea. A rise of the land north of the Gulf of Aquaba cut it off. The water began to evaporate leaving a great depression. It stretches for about 300km from just above the Sea of Galilee to some 70km south of the Dead Sea. The Dead Sea itself which is almost 400m below the level of the Mediterranean is the last remnant of this. It is also the lowest point on earth. Almost all the Jordan valley is more than 200m below sea level — the Sea of Galilee being minus 210m.

The Jordan river has washed salt down into the Dead Sea where its high concentration makes the Sea totally sterile and accounts for its name. The Sea of Galilee on the other hand is fresh water. The high concentration of salt in the Dead Sea accounts for its exceptional buoyancy. When the Roman emperor Vespasian heard of this he had some Jewish prisoners thrown into the water to see if they would float.

The hill country

The Jordan valley is separated from the coastal plain by a ridge of hills about 30km wide and about 130km long. This ridge forms a barrier rising about 500m above the level of the Mediterranean.

To the east of the Jordan limestone hills rise steeply to form a plateau 4–500m above sea level. To the north west of Galilee rises Mt Meron (1208m) and to the north-east the mass of Mt Hermon which is almost twice this height. In the south the country gives way to desert inhabited only by the Bedouin.

The desert and the fertile lands

The rainfall chart shows that over most of Palestine the rainfall is governed by the height of the land. On the central ridge the annual rainfall is 60–70cm and a little lower on the coastal plain. This is sufficient to make the land reasonably arable. East of the central ridge the land falls away rapidly and the lack of rainfall has turned the area into a desert — the Judaean wilderness.

Beyond the Jordan the hills rise again and the area enjoys a climate similar to the central ridge. The rainfall reaches 100cm in Galilee making it the most fertile area. But in the south the rainfall decreases and the desert sets in.

Map of Israel showing its rainfall. The highest rainfall is recorded on the highlands – particularly in northern Galilee and Mt. Hermon. The rainfall increases as one moves eastwards from the coast but after one has passed the centre of the ridge it decreases rapidly and the country gives way to near desert. This is particularly noticeable when one travels from Jerusalem to Jericho. The red line marks the area below sea level. The Dead Sea is 395 metres below the Mediterranean and is the lowest point on earth. The chart shows the annual rainfall in centimetres.

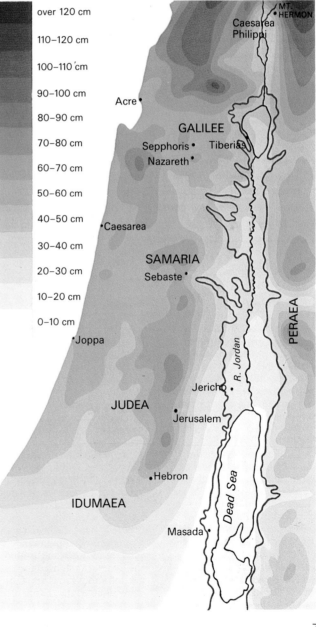

over 120 cm
110–120 cm
100–110 cm
90–100 cm
80–90 cm
70–80 cm
60–70 cm
50–60 cm
40–50 cm
30–40 cm
20–30 cm
10–20 cm
0–10 cm

MT. HERMON
Caesarea Philippi
Acre
GALILEE
Sepphoris • Tiberias
Nazareth •
Caesarea
SAMARIA
Sebaste •
Joppa
PERAEA
R. Jordan
Jericho
JUDEA
Jerusalem
Hebron
Dead Sea
IDUMAEA
Masada •

Alexander Jannaeus

In 103 BC the barbarous Alexander Jannaeus became king and under him the Jewish realm reached its greatest extent. But the collapse of Syria had encouraged the rise of other independent states. About 90 BC Alexander tried to extend his power in the north-east. Here he was defeated by the Nabataeans, lost his entire army, and his defeat triggered a rebellion at home led by the Pharisees. Alexander put down the revolt with great savagery. He crucified 800 of his opponents in front of his palace at Jerusalem where he and the women of his harem could watch them die in agony.

Alexander died in 76 BC to the great joy of his people. He was succeeded by his wife Salome, an intelligent and moderate woman who managed to bring order to her realm. Salome made peace with the Pharisees but it was a peace that could not last.

It was during Salome's reign that Herod was born. His father, Antipater, was a close friend of Hyrcanus Salome's elder son. Hyrcanus was a mild youth – a true son of Salome – but his brother Aristobulus was cast in the same vicious mould as his father. When Hyrcanus succeeded to the throne in 67 BC his brother, backed by the Sadducees, immediately led a revolt against him. At this point the history of the middle east abruptly changed course.

Rocks and soils

The hills of the central ridge, western Galilee, Perea and Mt. Carmel are mainly limestone. The soil is generally of the Mediterranean brown or terra rossa type ideally suitable for growing the olives which were so important as a source of oil. In southern Idumaea the soil gradually deteriorates and the Negev desert begins. East of the central ridge the rich soil gives way to the less fertile rendzina and finally to the inorganic dusty marl of the Judean wilderness. It consists of rocky hills and pale brown lifeless soil strewn with stones. In Galilee the soil is very fertile. The area around the Sea of Galilee stands out in stark contrast to the rest of the Jordan valley. The hillsides are strewn with black basalt boulders.

A fertile land

In ancient times there was far more woodland and undergrowth in Palestine. There was abundant wild life – wild boars, antelope, wolves, bears, even lions and, of course, lizards and snakes.

Wheat grew on the coastal plain and beyond the Jordan. Barley was grown in Idumaea. The hill country of Galilee, Samaria and Judea produced abundant fruit – in particular olives, grapes and figs. The lower Jordan valley was famous for its dates. The valleys were generally cultivated and the hillsides turned over to grazing sheep and goats. The near desert land to the south of Idumaea and around the Dead Sea was used for grazing sheep and goats. Cattle were raised on the coastal plain and west of the Sea of Galilee.

Ascalon

Anthedon

Gaza

N E G E V D

Model of Palestine showing the topography of the country. The country is split in two by the Jordan valley which is an extension of the Great Rift valley. For most of its length the Jordan valley is separated from the coastal plain by a limestone ridge rising some 600 metres above sea level.

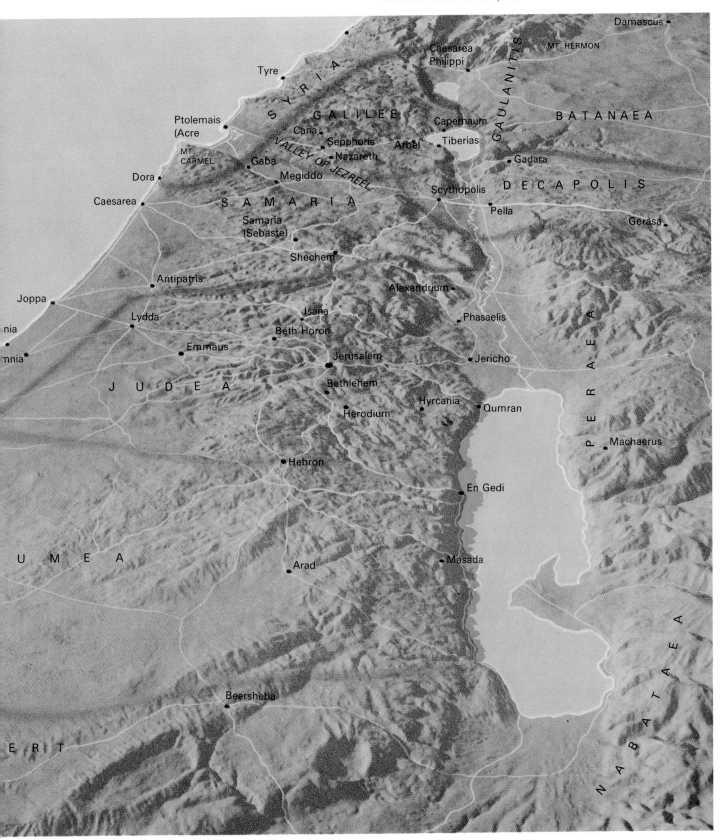

Damascus

MT. HERMON

Caesarea
Philippi

Tyre

GAULANITIS

BATANAEA

S Y R I A

GALILEE

Capernaum

Ptolemais
(Acre

Cana

Sepphoris

Tiberias

VALLEY OF JEZREEL

Nazareth

Arbel

MT.
CARMEL

Gaba

Gadara

Dora

Megiddo

DECAPOLIS

Scythopolis

Caesarea

S A M A R I A

Pella

Gerasa

Samaria
(Sebaste)

Shechem

Antipatris

Alexandrium

Joppa

Phasaelis

nia

Lydda

Isana

P
E
R
A
E
A

mnia

Beth Horon

Emmaus

Jerusalem

Jericho

Bethlehem

Hyrcania

Qumran

Herodium

U M E A

Hebron

Machaerus

En Gedi

Arad

Masada

N
A
B
A
T
A
E
A

Beersheba

E R T

9

The coming of Rome

For more than a hundred years before Herod's flight from Jerusalem Rome had been dabbling in eastern affairs. Rome set up and dethroned kings as she saw fit. In 67 BC Pompey, the greatest Roman general of his day, thrust eastwards crushing all before him. He advanced as far as the Caspian Sea and then turned south-west into Syria which was in a state of anarchy.

The brothers Hyrcanus and Aristobulus, rivals for the Hasmonaean lands, both sought Pompey's help. The Roman sided with Hyrcanus, the weaker of the two, and the easier to control. Bitterly disappointed Aristobulus seized Jerusalem. Pompey advanced on the city and Aristobulus retreated to the Temple which was built like a fortress. It fell after a seige of three months in 63 BC.

Pompey had heard a great deal about this Temple which only priests were allowed to enter. His curiosity got the better of him and he and his staff went into the Temple and even entered the Holy of Holies which the Jews believed was the throne-room of God. The Romans touched nothing but the Jews never forgave Pompey nor forgot his sacrilege.

Once again the Jews lost their liberty. The empire of the Hasmonaeans was broken up. Judea became a puppet of Rome. Samaria and the coastal strip which had been constantly ravaged by the Jewish kings were taken away and Hyrcanus was allowed to rule a much reduced realm. Syria became a Roman province whose governor was virtual overlord of Judea.

The Jews never accepted the Roman settlement. Within a short while they were up in arms again, and in 57 BC Gabinius the Governor of Syria had to help Hyrcanus put down the revolt. He divided the Jewish state into five self-governing districts. Hyrcanus remained in power in Jerusalem but even here he ruled only in name. Real power now rested in the hands of his chief minister Antipater – Herod's father.

Antipater realized that his only hope of keeping command lay in playing up to the Romans. But this was going to be difficult. War clouds were gathering. The new Parthian empire threatened the east and in Rome civil war seemed inevitable.

The hills of Judea to the south of Jerusalem. Bethlehem sprawls across the hills in the distance with the volcano-shaped fortress, Herodium, behind it. Beyond this is the Judean wilderness.

Judea

Greater Judea stretched from the level of Shechem in the north to the Negev desert in the south and from the Jordan valley in the east to the sea coast in the west. Pompey detached the mainly Greek-speaking area along the coast but left Idumaea as part of Judea. The coastal area was returned to Herod in 30 BC and from then on remained part of Judea.

Judea was a country of startling contrasts. The flat coastal plain is gradually engulfed by the wooded hills of the central ridge. These in turn give way to the Judean desert along the Jordan valley and the Dead Sea. South of Hebron the country slowly deteriorates into the Negev desert.

The coastal plain provided abundant wheat harvests and grazing land. Olives and vines grew on the hills. These were interspersed with fig trees and the Egyptian sycamore which bore a fig-like fruit. Even the Judean desert was not completely barren and supported flocks of sheep. The area

around the oasis of Jericho produced date palms, famous for the strength of their wine and balsam which was prized both as a medicine and a perfume.

ABOVE: the startlingly beautiful Judean wilderness seen from the fortress, Hyrcania. It was here that Jesus fasted for 40 days before beginning his preaching.

BELOW: a map of Judea showing the roads. The Judean wilderness is to the east of the main north-south road that runs through Jerusalem.

In the wake of Caesar

By 55 BC the Roman empire was controlled by three men: Pompey, Crassus and Julius Caesar. Each swore to help the other two. Caesar had acquired the provinces north of Italy and had already set out on his famous conquest of Gaul. Pompey had been given Spain. Crassus, fabled for his wealth and greed, became governor of Syria. He saw himself as the new Alexander the Great. Before he set out on the conquest of the world he stole the treasure of the Temple in Jerusalem and the Jews considered it divine retribution when both he and his army were destroyed by the Parthians.

After Crassus' death Pompey and Caesar realised that the world was not big enough for both of them. Caesar seized Italy and Pompey retreated to the east. Caesar followed, defeated him decisively, and Pompey fled to Egypt where he was assassinated.

In the closing stages of Rome's civil war Herod's father, Antipater had supported Julius Caesar. In gratitude Caesar restored his master, Hyrcanus to his position as ruler of the Jews. Antipater himself was given the official title of procurator of Judea.

Caesar left his cousin Sextus as governor of Syria and returned to Rome. Antipater's position was now much stronger and he was able to give important positions to his two eldest sons. Phasael was made governor of Jerusalem and Herod, now about 25 years old, was given command over Galilee.

The Galileans were fiercely independent and Herod showed little mercy in establishing his authority. He was called before the council at Jerusalem, the Sanhedrin, which was dominated by his enemies and charged with illegally executing his opponents. On the advice of his father Herod took his bodyguard with him. The Sanhedrin felt powerless to condemn him but Herod believed his life was in danger and left the country. He never forgot this humiliation. He withdrew to Syria where Sextus put him in charge of the border zones next to Judea.

Julius Caesar's patronage did not last long. In 44 BC the Roman world was again thrown into turmoil when Caesar was murdered by Brutus and Cassius and civil war broke out again. Brutus, Cassius and the other assassins took control of the east. Antipater was forced to do another about face. He had to prove to his masters what a good ally he could be. But hardly had the Jews settled to the new regime when there was another change of course.

Samaria

Central Samaria was very similar to Judea with vineyards and olive groves clothing its hills. In the west were extensive forests. Here oaks and terebinths grew. There were also carobs, pistacchios and oriental plane trees rising out of a dense undergrowth of myrtle, broom and other bushes such as acanthus, wormwood and asphodel. To the north was the plain of Jezreel which was rich in wheat. It separated Samaria from Galilee.

Galilee

Galilee was the most fertile area of Palestine. It has a sub-tropical climate with a plentiful rainfall. The Jewish historian Josephus claims that virtually anything will grow there. Although it abounds with date palms, figs and olives, the walnut which usually prefers a colder climate also grows there. It was well-known for its wheat-fields and vineyards. Red wine was very popular with the Jews.

Galilee was the main area for growing flax, from which linen was made. Sepphoris the capital of Galilee was the linen centre of Palestine. The Sea of Galilee, which is in fact a fresh water lake, had a plentiful supply of fish. Galilee is cut off from the Mediterranean by Phoenicia, the most southerly part of the province of Syria.

ABOVE TOP: view looking south-east from Sebaste the capital of Samaria. The landscape is very similar to that of Judea. In the distance in the centre is Mt. Gerizim where the Samaritans built their Temple.

ABOVE: the north-west shore of the Sea of Galilee in the spring. The Golan hills are in the distance.

LEFT: the valley of Jezreel in the spring. It is seen from Megiddo looking north. Nazareth, now a sprawling town, can be seen on the distant hills in the centre. Mt. Tabor is to the right of it. The plain in front of Megiddo is famous as the place where the prophesied ultimate battle of Armageddon will be fought.

RIGHT: typical rich Galilean summer flora. This stands in stark contrast to the rest of Palestine.

The invasion of the Parthians

The instability of the Roman empire encouraged Hyrcanus' rivals to make another bid for power. Herod's father was murdered and Hyrcanus' nephew Antigonus, Aristobulus' son, invaded the country with Parthian support. Herod was recalled to help deal with the situation and successfully repelled the invaders. He was given a rapturous welcome by Hyrcanus who betrothed him to his beautiful granddaughter Miriam. Herod was already married. But this new marriage would give him the respectability that he needed. He divorced his wife Doris and expelled her and Antipater their son from Jerusalem.

Just as Herod's fortunes seemed to be rising came the news of the defeat of Brutus and Cassius by Mark Antony and Caesar's nephew, Octavian. Antony now became ruler of the east. Hyrcanus was forced to do yet another about face. Accompanied by Phasael and Herod he went cap in hand with bags of money to make peace with his new master. Antony desperately needed all the support he could get as he was expecting an attack by the Parthians. Hyrcanus was once again confirmed in his position and Phasael and Herod were given the title 'tetrarch'.

Among the many monarchs who appeared before Antony to swear their allegiance was Cleopatra, queen of Egypt. Her legendary charm and wit were not wasted on Antony. When Cleopatra returned to Egypt, Antony followed.

Antony spent the winter of 41/40 BC in Cleopatra's arms. In the spring the Parthians invaded Syria. Once in the province part of their army turned south into Judea. In a concerted effort Antigonus, Hyrcanus' nephew, also invaded Judea and made a dash for Jerusalem. The brothers Herod and Phasael tried to head him off but he managed to seize the Temple precinct. Soon after the Parthian army also arrived.

Everything had happened so quickly that the Parthian general was unsure what to do. He suggested that Hyrcanus and Phasael should put their case to his commander-in-chief. They were conducted to the Parthian headquarters and there arrested. Phasael, knowing full well what Antigonus would do to him, committed suicide. Hyrcanus survived but his nephew cut off his ears (some say that he bit them off) so that he could never be a high priest again. It was a Jewish law that anybody who was physically deformed could not hold the office of high priest.

Meanwhile Herod, foreseeing the worst, prepared to escape from Jerusalem before the Parthians tightened their security.

The Hasmonaean family tree. The dates given in brackets show how long each member ruled.
Jonathan made the Jews entirely independent of the Syrians and had himself made High Priest. His successors inherited the powerful High Priesthood.

The expansion of Judea
Before the revolt of the Maccabaeans against the Syrians the only area intensively occupied by the Jews was Judea itself. There were some Jewish settlements in the surrounding areas. Since the time of Alexander the Great a whole series of cities with Greek culture had sprung up all over the east. There were many in Palestine. Their inhabitants were mainly Greek-speaking Syrians.
The whole coastline was controlled by a string of these Greek cities. Joppa and Gazara were captured by Simon Maccabaeus. The inhabitants were converted and circumcised by force. Any who refused were expelled. Jamnia was also taken over. Alexander Jannaeus captured Gaza, Anthedon and Raphia but they were later given back their Greek status by Pompey.
John Hyrcanus conquered Idumaea and forcibly converted it. It remained Jewish and was annexed to Judea.

The chosen people

RIGHT: Mt. Gerizim which overlooks Shechem. At the end of the 4th century BC the Samaritans set up their Temple on top of the hill in opposition to the one at Jerusalem.

BELOW: A map of Palestine at the beginning of Herod's reign showing the various provinces. The Greek cities are marked in red.

The Galileans

Galilee was not a Jewish homeland but there were scattered Jewish settlements there. About 102 BC Aristobulus I invaded the country to protect the Jewish settlers who were in open conflict with their gentile neighbours. He forcibly converted the population and Jewish emigrants poured in from the south. Galilee was a frontier province bordering on Syria and much of the population remained gentile, at least in spirit. Like most frontiersmen the Galilean Jews were a hardened people. Although Galilee became predominantly Jewish it was prone to disturbances.

Beyond the Jordan

The area to the east of the river Jordan had been conquered by Alexander Jannaeus. Its Greek cities – Hippus, Gadara, Pella, Dium, Gerasa and Philadelphia had been restored by Pompey and his lieutenant Gabinius. They remained Greek in culture but the area, particularly near the Jordan, became predominantly Jewish.

East of Galilee

To the east of the sea of Galilee were the provinces of Gaulanitis, Batanea, Trachonitis and Auranitis. There were Jewish settlements here but the population was predominantly Syrian with a mixture of nomadic Arab types. By comparison Galilee was a peaceful area. Alexander Jannaeus had tried to conquer the area but had been driven out by the Nabataean king, Obodas. The area was finally given to Herod by the Romans.

Samaria

The Samaritans were a mixed population. Gentiles had been settled in the area by the Assyrians (C700 BC). They had intermarried with the Jewish population and accepted their religion.

When the Jews returned from exile in the 6th century BC they refused to allow the Samaritans, whom they considered an impure race, to help rebuild the Temple in Jerusalem. Relations between the two communities grew worse and, at the end of the 4th century, the Samaritans built their own Temple on Mt. Gerizim. This resulted in the great schism. A bitter hatred developed which may be compared with the conflict between Catholic and Protestant existing in some areas today. Alexander the Great had established a colony of his troops in the city of Samaria. It was destroyed by John Hyrcanus but rebuilt as a Greek city by Pompey's lieutenant, Gabinius and enlarged by Herod.

Outside influences

Greek culture had a great impact on the Jews despite their resistance to it. It even permeated their extremist sects such as the Essenes. There was another Jewish population which probably outnumbered the million or so living in Palestine. Jews had emigrated over the centuries and lived in many of the cities of the Eastern Roman Empire. This was known as the Diaspora (dispersion). They had adopted the Greek language and culture. Their largest community was at Alexandria, and many Jews still lived in Babylon.

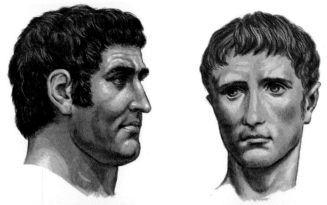

King of the Jews

On the first news of the Parthian invasion in 40 BC Antony left Egypt and sailed north to Tyre. But there was nothing he could do. He sailed on to Asia Minor (Turkey) and then to Greece where he took stock of the situation. The mass of his troops were in the west where, he had just learned, hostilities had broken out with Caesar's nephew and adopted son Octavian. Antony immediately sailed for Italy where Octavian opposed his landing. It seemed that the civil war would flare up again but the veterans on both sides welcomed each other and the heat was taken out of the situation. A new treaty was concluded and Octavian sealed the pact by giving his sister Octavia to Antony in marriage.

Herod had arrived in Egypt in the autumn. He had then followed Antony to Asia Minor and then on to Italy. In Rome he appealed to Antony for help against Antigonus, backing up his plea with a large sum of money. Although the money helped, Antony recognised in Herod the only person who could possibly govern Judea and prove a reliable bastion against the Parthians. He managed to convince Octavian and the senate. Herod was nominated king of Judea. Flanked by Antony and Octavian Herod mounted the Capitol where he offered sacrifice to Jupiter. This, Herod's first act as king, was to characterise his reign. For although he observed Jewish law in Judea he was only half Jewish and a gentile at heart.

Wasting no time Herod sailed back to the east and landed at Acre in southern Syria. He was concerned for his relatives at the fortress of Masada which had been under siege ever since he had left. Reduced to dire straits through lack of water, they had been saved by a downpour which had filled the cisterns. He collected a considerable force and with the support of the Romans advanced on Galilee. Having secured his communications Herod pushed down the coast to Joppa. Once he had gained control of the port he was able to march into Idumaea and relieve Masada.

He now turned north to Jerusalem, planning to lay siege to the city. It was mid-winter and the Roman commander insisted on withdrawing his troops to winter quarters because of lack of supplies. The historian Josephus claims he was bribed. Herod attempted to bring up provisions from Samaria but the Romans refused to close in.

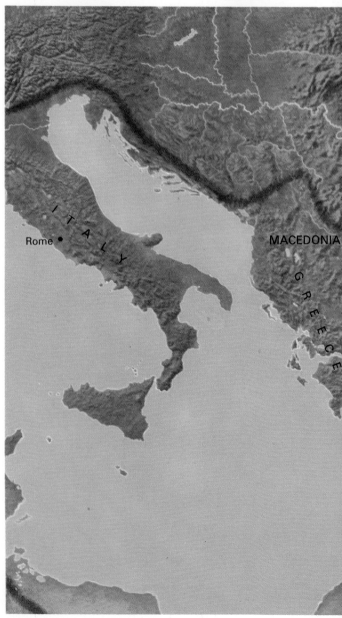

A Roman vassal

Herod had been made King of the Jews and owed allegiance to Rome. He was left free to run his kingdom as he saw fit. If he had made a mess of it he would have been deposed. Only his foreign policy had to be approved by Rome.

Herod's position was not unique. He was one of many such rulers. The Romans had never really gloried in the idea of empire. They conquered countries for various reasons. Self-defence had been the original motive but during the two centuries before Herod's rule greed and glory played an ever increasing role. Glory had become the prime motive for conquest and greed the reason for governing the provinces.

Client kings

During 150 years before Herod's reign it had become the Roman custom to place a friendly king on the throne of any country on their borders that they had no wish to govern. The Romans called these rulers 'client kings'. Often the original king was left in command; sometimes he was removed and another more acceptable to Rome, took over. The Romans established a vast number of these petty kingdoms along their frontiers. They acted as 'buffers' against Rome's more powerful enemies. Rome had gradually absorbed the sea board of the eastern Mediterranean establishing client states and then gobbling them up.

The lot of an ally

Once the Romans had interfered in the affairs of another state or agreed to an alliance with it they considered it to be entirely at their disposal. A state was not allowed to back out of such an arrangement. Any attempt to do so would be considered rebellion. This often came as a shock to 'friendly' states who misunderstood what being a friend of Rome really meant.

A king who had become an ally voluntarily could find himself deposed on the slightest pretext and replaced by another ruler or even a Roman governor. Client rulers of very minor states were refused the title of king and called tetrarchs.

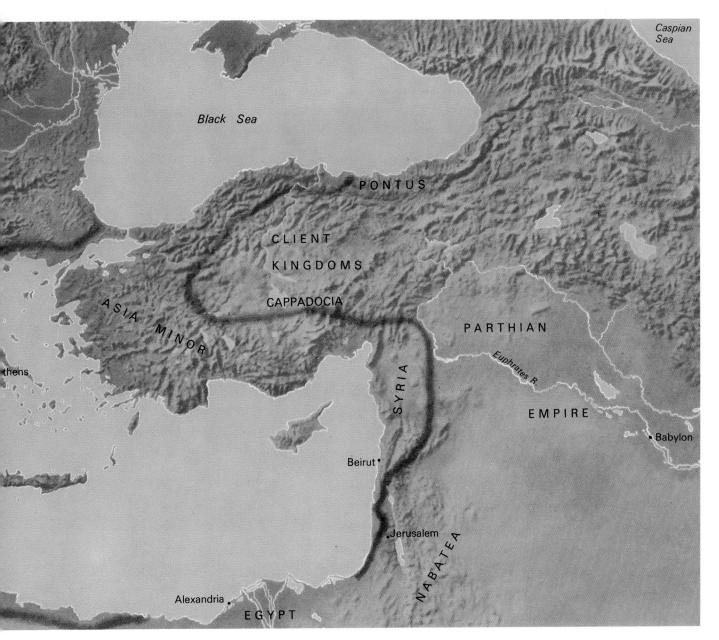

The struggle for Judea

Denied a quick victory in Jerusalem Herod decided to subdue the countryside. He marched north into Galilee and stormed its capital Sepphoris. The country offered little resistance but a band of guerrillas took refuge in the caves of Arbel just west of the Sea of Galilee. These caves are half way up a sheer cliff face and Herod was forced to lower his men in baskets over the edge to come to grips with them. Using grappling hooks they were able to dislodge most of the defenders. The remainder were burned out.

Herod now moved south into Samaria but was forced to turn back to suppress a rebellion. He put down the revolt ruthlessly, slaughtering the rebels, destroying their strongholds and plundering the countryside. Meanwhile, his Roman allies who had gone to help the governor of Syria, decisively defeated the Parthians in June 38 BC.

Soon after Antony arrived in the east. Herod now received the help of two legions, commanded by the much more reliable Sosius and was at last able to start his long delayed march on Jerusalem. In the early winter of 38/37 BC he was able to bring some of Antigonus' troops to battle some 30km north of the city and decisively defeat them. The remains of Antigonus' army fled to Isana. Herod following up burst into the town. In their fury his troops tore down the houses and butchered the soldiers inside.

The following spring, before laying siege to Jerusalem, Herod married Miriam. He had been engaged to her for five years. He hoped that his marrying into the Hasmonaean family would make him more acceptable to the people of Jerusalem.

Once Sosius arrived with his troops the siege of Jerusalem began in earnest. The north side of the city was protected by two walls, and the first assault was against the outer one. In an attempt to collapse the defences the Romans undermined stretches of the wall and brought up their battering rams. The Jews fought back with grim determination. They tried to fire the siege engines and when they failed, broke into the mines and fought the Romans hand to hand underground. But against the superior Roman training and technique they stood no real chance.

For six weeks the Jews held the outer wall. When it was finally stormed they retreated to the inner wall. Here they held out for a further two weeks. Once over this barrier the Romans burst into the lower city, cutting Jerusalem in half. Some of the defenders fled to the Temple whilst the rest took refuge in the upper city. Still hoping to avoid a massacre and reach terms Herod sent sacrificial animals into the Temple so that the daily sacrifices could be continued. But it was to no avail. The Roman troops, frustrated by the length of the siege, could be held back no longer. Herod's Jewish forces, filled with the excesses of hatred that are born of civil war, were equally impatient for the final assault. Both the Temple and the upper city were stormed. Neither women, children nor old people were spared. Herod managed to prevent the desecration of the Temple and begged Sosius to call off his troops before the city was totally destroyed. Herod said that he wanted a kingdom to rule, not a desert. Antigonus was sent to Antony and later executed. So the Hasmonaean dynasty came to an end and in the summer of 37 BC Herod mounted the blood-spattered throne.

The hills of Arbel just west of the Sea of Galilee. The cliffs are honeycombed with caves. The Galileans opposed to Herod took refuge in here. Herod was only able to get at them by lowering his men down the cliff face in 'cradles' and smoking them out.

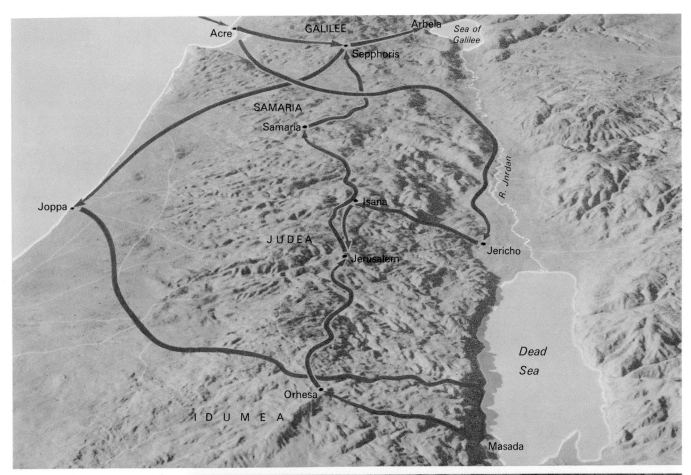

ABOVE: a map showing Herod's campaigns against Antigonus from 39–37 BC. Joppa was in enemy hands so he landed at Ptolemais (Acre). This was in the province of Syria. Although it was winter he marched on Galilee. He then stormed Joppa and marched to the relief of his family at Masada.

He advanced on Jerusalem and with the help of the Romans laid siege to the city. But the Romans were bribed to discontinue the siege. Herod marched north and took Sepphoris during a snow storm. The Galileans fled to the caves at Arbel and he was forced to winkle them out.

In the summer of 38 BC he received reliable Roman support. He defeated Antigonus' army at Isana and advanced to besiege Jerusalem again.

RIGHT: Herod's siege of Jerusalem. The attack was launched against the north wall which was the weakest point. The Jews were no match for the Romans. The wall fell in 40 days. The inner wall fell 15 days later. Herod now attacked the Temple and the Romans the upper city.
1 Temple. 2 Bira fortress.

The mailed fist

Herod immediately set about making his throne secure. Ten years earlier the Sanhedrin had charged him with a capital offence. Now he was to have his revenge. The council was dominated by the Saducees who had been the chief supporters of Antigonus. Herod executed 45 of its 70 members and confiscated their property. It made a welcome addition to his treasury. The power of the council was henceforth restricted to religious matters. Sosius left one legion behind in Judea but it could not remain indefinitely.

Herod established a string of fortresses and military colonies throughout the country to secure his position.

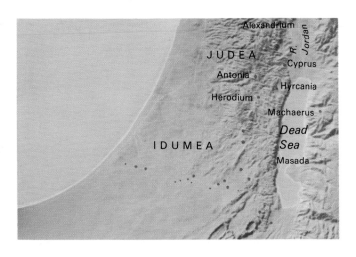

ABOVE: map of Judea, Idumaea and Perea showing Herod's fortresses (large red dots) and watch towers (small dots).

LEFT: the site of Hyrcania in the Judean desert. The fortress was built on top of the cone-shaped hill.

BOTTOM LEFT: the site of Alexandrium in the Jordan valley – the highest of the fortresses. It was on top of the hill in the centre.

Herod's border defences
Immediately he had secured his kingdom Herod began its fortification. A string of fortresses were built or rebuilt along his eastern border. Although these were used to control his own subjects their prime purpose was as a defence against the Nabatean Arabs. Among these fortresses were Alexandrium, and Cyprus named after Herod's mother, which was built overlooking Jericho and guarding the road to Jerusalem. On the east side of the Dead Sea was Machaerus, notorious as the place where John the Baptist was executed. Further down the Dead Sea on the west side he fortified the rock of Masada. Along his southern borders he erected a string of forts and watch towers.

Herod's internal defences

Herod built several fortresses which were used primarily to control his subjects. The most famous of these were the Bira at Jerusalem, and Hyrcania in the Judean desert. Herod remodelled the Bira and renamed it Antonia in honour of Antony (see p. 87). Hyrcania was also an existing fortress. Under Herod it became notorious as a place where trouble makers were taken, and never heard of again.

Later in his reign (c20 BC) Herod built a unique fortress which he named Herodium. This is near Bethlehem. It was a fortified palace like Masada and the Bira. The round fortress was reinforced by three semi-circular towers and one much taller round one.

ABOVE: the site of Herodium. Herod's fortified palace was built on the hill which had had the top cut off. After it was built the earth was piled up against the walls to make a steep slope.

BELOW: a reconstruction of the fortified palace at Herodium. The round tower probably housed heavy catapults. This tower had a solid base so that the recoil of the catapults would not shake it to pieces. The palace was approached by an underground passageway with 200 steps leading up from the bottom of the hill **4**.

1 Colonnaded court
2 Synagogue
3 Bathrooms

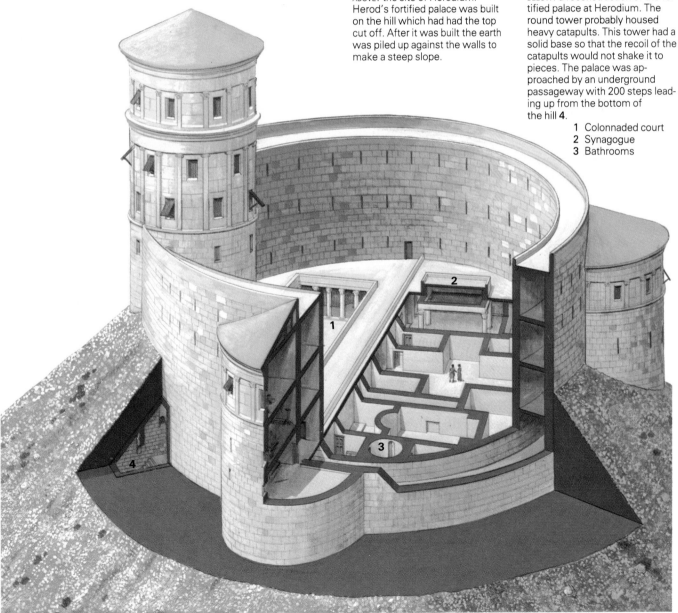

Antony and Cleopatra

After making peace with Octavian, Antony moved east bringing his new wife Octavia with him. She tried hard to keep the pleasure loving Antony on a straight course and for a while she succeeded. But whilst Herod was finally securing his throne in Jerusalem a new conflict flared up between Antony and Octavian. Octavia managed to bring the two men together again but it seems to have entirely destroyed Antony's affection for her. Octavia's sober life had begun to bore him and his thoughts drifted back to Egypt and Cleopatra. He had not seen her for nearly four years. Octavia was expecting a child so Antony sent her back to Rome. He then summoned Cleopatra to Antioch in Syria and married her. Octavian was furious at the insult to himself and his family.

The marriage was also a terrible blow to Herod. He knew that Cleopatra wished to rebuild the empire of her fathers and that that empire had included Judea. He re-fortified Masada, and built palaces on the rock as a retreat for himself and his family in the event of an Egyptian invasion. Great cisterns were hewn out of the rock to collect the rain water so that it would be possible to hold out for years.

But although Antony was deeply in love he refused to give in to Cleopatra's wilder demands. The very fertile oasis of Jericho with its rich harvest of dates and Balsam was taken from Herod and given to the queen; insult was added to injury when she allowed Herod to rent it back from her. Other small sections of his lands were given to Cleopatra, but Herod managed to hold on to the bulk of his kingdom.

Herod had established his authority over the realm but in his home he was less successful. From the very beginning of his reign, domestic problems plagued him. With Antigonus dead it was necessary to nominate a new high priest. It had been customary under the Hasmonaeans for the king to be high priest as well but Herod's origins made this impossible. Hyrcanus had been released by the Parthians and Herod welcomed him back to Judea treating him with great honour. But Hyrcanus could never be high priest again. Antigonus had seen to that when he had 'bitten' off his ears. Herod would not place another Hasmonaean in the position for this would pose a constant threat to himself. So he looked around for a candidate of impeccable background but not of Hasmonaean descent. The man selected was Hananel a priest from the Jews at Babylon.

Snake
path

Defence against Cleopatra

Herod feared that Antony would give Cleopatra his kingdom. He decided to prepare a fortified retreat where, if his Roman ally turned on him, he could wait for better days. Masada towers some 400m above the western shore of the Dead Sea. He walled in the summit, dug water cisterns and moved up vast stores of food. He built two palaces with all the amenities to allay the boredom of a siege.

A reconstruction of Herod's great fortress at Masada seen from the north. There were only two ways up to the top: a short one from the west side (right) and the tortuous snake path up the east side (left).

1 Hanging Palace
2 Water Gate 3 Bath house
4 Storehouses 5 Synagogue
6 Western Palace
7 Ritual bath (Mikve)
8 Large underground cistern
9 Aqueduct to lower cisterns

The death of a high priest

Herod's decision to make Hananel high priest infuriated the Hasmonaean members of his family and household. He could argue that Hananel was a direct descendant of Zadok, who had been high priest at the time of Solomon, but this gained him nothing. His mother-in-law Alexandra wrote an angry letter to Cleopatra. She was sure that Cleopatra could persuade Antony to overrule Herod and transfer the high priesthood to her seventeen year old son Aristobulus. Miriam too used her charms to support her brother's cause. It was too much and Herod gave in. He sacked Hananel and made the young Aristobulus high priest.

Herod suspected that this was the first step in a plot to overthrow him and had his mother-in-law placed under surveillance. This infuriated Alexandra who plotted to escape to Cleopatra in Egypt with her son. Herod was informed of the plan but there was nothing he could do – at least openly. He pretended to forgive them, and bided his time.

At the feast of Tabernacles in 35 BC Aristobulus officiated as high priest for the first time. When the crowds saw the handsome youth in his sacred robes they were reminded of the regal position his family had once enjoyed and began to mumble against the usurper. When this was reported to Herod he decided to act immediately. The feast lasted for a week or more. When it was over the whole family went down to Jericho where they were entertained by Alexandra at her winter palace outside the town. Herod encouraged the young Aristobulus to get drunk and, as it was a very hot afternoon, took him for a stroll beside the swimming pools in the palace grounds. By arrangement some of Herod's young friends were romping in the water and the king urged Aristobulus to join the game. In pretence of play the youths ducked him and held him down until he drowned. Herod pretended to be appalled at the 'accident' and prepared an elaborate funeral for the boy. Alexandra guessed the truth. She said nothing to Herod but wrote again to her friend Cleopatra. On hearing of the accusation Antony summoned Herod to him.

In great trepidation Herod appeared before his patron, ready with excuses and the customary large sum of money. But his reception was not what he expected. Antony understood Herod's predicament. He did not even refer to the charges.

An impregnable fortress

Masada had once been part of the precipitous plateau that hems in the western side of the Dead Sea. Millions of years of erosion isolated it from the plateau and turned it into an impregnable fortress.

The rock was first fortified by the Hasmonaean kings but it was Herod who built the structures that can now be seen.

The defences

Masada could be approached only from the east or the west. On the east there is a tortuous and narrow track, 5.5km long, known as the snake path. It has to be climbed in single file under constant threat from above. On the western side it is less than 100m high. Herod surrounded the summit with a casemate wall – a wall with rooms in it. This was strengthened by towers mainly concentrated at the weak spots on the east and west sides.

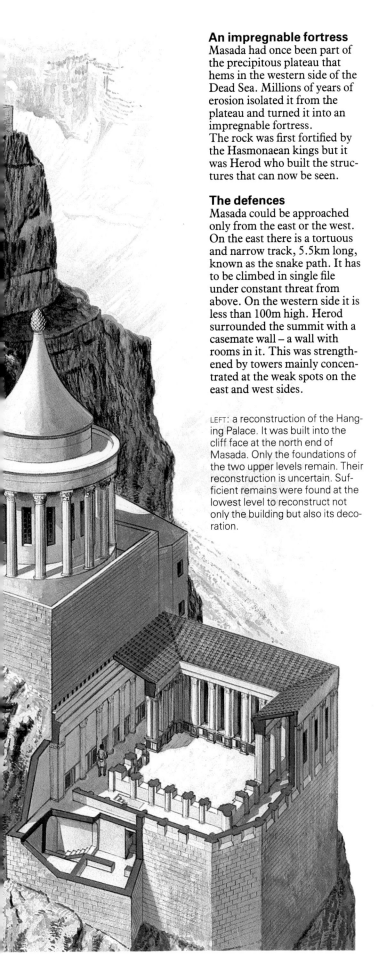

LEFT: a reconstruction of the Hanging Palace. It was built into the cliff face at the north end of Masada. Only the foundations of the two upper levels remain. Their reconstruction is uncertain. Sufficient remains were found at the lowest level to reconstruct not only the building but also its decoration.

ABOVE: a reconstruction of the decoration of the lowest level of the Hanging Palace. It is similar to the decoration of the same period at Pompeii. It consists of flat panels of colour interspersed with panels painted to look like marble.

Water supply

Herod's family had suffered from thirst during the Parthian siege of Masada. He was determined that this would not happen again. He cut two rows of cisterns in the rock face above the Ben Yair ravine which runs along the north west face of Masada. He then dammed the ravine and the Masada valley that runs round the south-west end of the fortress. He built simple aqueducts from them to the cisterns. The Ben Yair filled the lower row of cisterns and the Masada valley fed the upper row. In the rainy season the dams collected the water and it flowed along the aqueduct to the cisterns. These cisterns could hold about 40,000 cubic metres of water. The water was carried up a winding path, through the Water Gate and poured into vast cisterns on the summit.

The Hanging Palace

The most remarkable of Herod's buildings at Masada is the so-called 'Hanging Palace'. This was built into the north end of the rock at three levels. The top level was built on the summit but the two other levels were constructed in steps down the cliff face. The lowest level was 35m down the cliff face. The various levels were reached by square 'spiral' staircases. Unfortunately only the lowest level is sufficiently intact to make an accurate attempt at reconstruction. Here there was a colonnaded court with a small bathroom attached.

The inevitable disaster

Herod's troubles with his family were only just beginning. When he arrived back from his visit to Antony his sister Salome accused her husband Joseph of adultery with Miriam. Herod ever a jealous lover, in his rage had Joseph executed, but his passion for his beautiful wife was so great that he could not bear to condemn her. From this moment a bitter feud developed between Miriam and Salome. Each was backed up by her mother. Their continuous feud was to make Herod's life complete misery.

Meanwhile the Roman world was again heading for upheaval. Relations between Antony and Octavian had been growing steadily worse. Cleopatra's influence over Antony was resented at Rome where Octavia, his long-suffering wife, was greatly loved. Amidst increasing hostility Antony started to mobilise his forces. He and Cleopatra moved to Ephesus on the eastern side of the Aegean Sea in the autumn of 33 BC, and began massing their troops. Herod warned Antony against Cleopatra. He could not believe that Antony's legions would fight for Cleopatra against their own countrymen. Herod's advice was simple and ruthless: 'Kill her and annexe Egypt.'

The following spring Antony's troops moved into Greece. Here he made his final commitment to Cleopatra and his worst mistake. He divorced Octavia and had her thrown out of his house in Rome. Rumour that he intended to transfer the capital of the empire from Rome to Alexandria just added fuel to the fire. His troops, officers and men, began to desert him. In the winter of 32/31 BC Rome declared war – not on Antony but on 'the eastern harlot'.

The two sides came into conflict the following summer. In the face of continued desertions Antony decided on a naval battle at Actium. At the height of the battle, seeing victory slipping from her grasp, Cleopatra raised her sails and fled back to Egypt. Antony followed. Here, deserted by his forces, he stabbed himself and died in his lover's arms. Cleopatra tried to bargain with Octavian, offering her own life for the children she had borne Antony. In the end she too committed suicide. The only person to come out of this story untarnished is Octavia. She adopted the children Antony had by Cleopatra and brought them up as her own.

An aerial view of the Western Palace at Masada seen from the north-east.
1 The service wing
2 The royal quarters
3 The storerooms
4 The administration wing

Other palaces at Masada
The Hanging Palace is not the only royal accommodation on Masada. There was also a far larger palace in the centre of the west side and three other buildings which might be described as palaces. These smaller buildings might have been for Herod's own family and his wife's family who hated each other so much that they had to be kept separate.

The Western Palace
This is the largest palace at Masada. The royal quarters are in the south-east corner (top left corner of the photograph on the left). To the right of these were the storerooms. In the north-east wing (bottom left) were kitchens, workshops etc., and opposite them the administrative building.
The decoration is not as well preserved as in the hanging Palace, but two beautiful mosaic floors were discovered in the area of Herod's private bathroom which are under the large roof on the left of the photograph.

Herod's private bath

In the royal quarters of the Western Palace the archaeologists uncovered Herod's private bathrooms. These are of Graeco-Roman type. They are the best preserved rooms in the palace. Their mosaic floors are almost intact.

The bathrooms contain a changing room with a fine mosaic in it. This leads off to a small warm room, which in turn leads into a hot room. This has a bath set in an alcove at the far end. The room and the water are heated by a furnace behind the bath. On the other side of the changing room steps lead down to a cold plunge bath.

The public bathhouse

Just behind the Hanging Palace is a public bathhouse. This is a typical Graeco-Roman installation with cold, warm and hot rooms. It was probably built primarily for Herod's foreign visitors. There are similar baths at the palaces at Jericho and Herodium.

The decoration in the changing room and warm room are well preserved.

ABOVE: Herod's private bathrooms in the Western Palace.
1 Changing room
2 Warm room
3 The hot room with bath
4 Stairs leading down to the cold bath

LEFT: bathhouse utensils from Pompeii. The hot room made the bather perspire. The curved strigils were used to scrape the skin down. The little jar contained oil which was used to massage the bather.

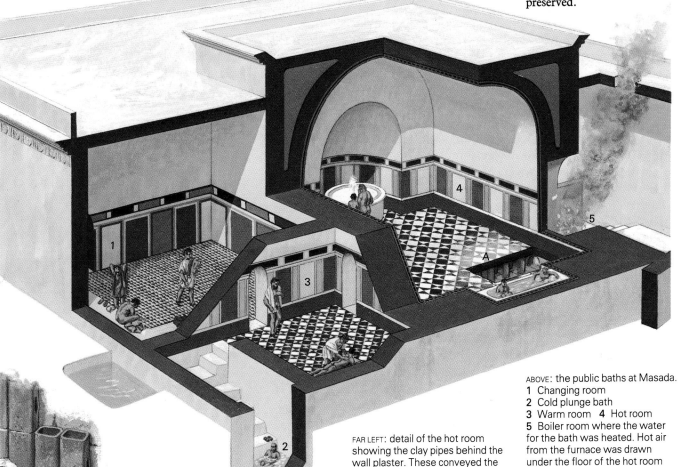

FAR LEFT: detail of the hot room showing the clay pipes behind the wall plaster. These conveyed the hot air up the walls to heat the whole room.

ABOVE: the public baths at Masada.
1 Changing room
2 Cold plunge bath
3 Warm room   4 Hot room
5 Boiler room where the water for the bath was heated. Hot air from the furnace was drawn under the floor of the hot room which was raised on small columns (see cutaway A).

Judaism and its priests

Another about-face

Pompey, Caesar, Cassius, Antony and now Octavian. Once again Herod had a new master. He had not been directly involved in the war. He had prepared a force to support Antony but it had been diverted. A few years earlier Antony had imposed a tribute on the Nabataean Arabs. This tribute was to be paid to Cleopatra who had insisted that Herod collect it for her. When Antony's power declined the Arabs refused to pay the tribute. Herod had been ordered to use his troops to collect it. It was a bad time for Herod. His campaign against the Nabataeans was far from glorious. In his absence Judea was devastated by an earthquake in 31 BC. Thousands died and a vast amount of property and livestock was destroyed. The Essene monastery at Qumran was badly damaged and for a while deserted.

Herod knew that he must confront Octavian as soon as possible but before doing so he wanted to secure his own position. There was only one person who now posed a threat to him – the ageing Hyrcanus. The old man had no desire for political power and was content to live out the remainder of his days in peace. But not so his daughter Alexandra. She had a burning desire for vengeance over the death of her young son whom Herod had drowned. She urged the old man to reclaim the throne. In the face of this threat Herod charged the ex-king with treason and had him executed. Now Herod was ready to meet Octavian.

In case things went wrong Herod sent his mother, his sister Salome, and his children to the fortress at Masada. It was impossible to send Miriam and Alexandra to the same place because of their feud with Salome so they were sent to the fortress of Alexandrium overlooking the Jordan valley. Herod's ungovernable passion for Miriam made the thought of her marrying anyone else after his death unthinkable. He therefore gave secret orders that if anything happened to him she should be killed.

Leaving his brother Pheroras in charge, Herod sailed for Rhodes to meet Octavian. He took a large sum of money as a present for his new master. Herod removed his crown before the meeting but made no apology for supporting Antony. In fact he stressed his loyalty to his former patron and asked for the opportunity to prove as loyal a friend to Octavian. The new ruler of the world was impressed by Herod's forthright approach and handed him back his crown. Once again Herod had survived.

ABOVE: a mosaic from the Synagogue at Beth Alpha, Israel. It shows Abraham in the linen garment of a priest.

BELOW: a reconstruction of a ritual bath (mikve) at Masada. A ritual bath had to be part filled with pure rain water that had flowed into it. The correct volume could be made up from water carried to it.
1 Channel for rain water
2 Rain water tank
3 The actual bath
4 Pool for washing hands and feet before bathing

Judaism
In its simplest form the Jewish religion (Judaism) consisted of worshipping a single god (Jahweh) and obeying his law (the Torah) which had been revealed to Moses. This law regulated the whole of Jewish life.

Impurity
Judaism laid down precise laws on impurity. This has no connection with the Christian idea of impurity. It was the result of contamination. A Jew had to avoid coming into contact with someone or something contaminated. For example idolatry, mildew in houses or on pots and cups, touching a dead animal or human, and certain sexual practices caused contamination. A woman who had had a baby was contaminated. Once contaminated a Jew was untouchable and had to be cleansed. It would be a serious sin for a Jew to perform acts such as eating holy food whilst impure. Cleansing was also necessary after a holy act. A priest who had offered sacrifice was untouchable. It was necessary to wash away the contamination. Different sorts of contamination required different methods and periods of purification. These consisted of waiting anything up to 80 days and then bathing in ritually pure water, washing one's clothes and offering sacrifice.

Sacrifices

All sacrifices were offered by the priests at the altar in front of the Temple at Jerusalem. An offering could consist of an animal, vegetable or incense. Communal sacrifice was offered in the morning and evening. Special sacrifices were offered at festivals and other important days such as Sabbaths. Priests also offered sacrifices for individuals. These were to express joy or sadness or to fulfil vows. Normally the offering would be eaten by the offerer and the priests. Certain parts of the sacrifice were always burned. The blood of the victim belonged to Jahweh and was sprinkled on the altar. The poor could only afford to sacrifice birds. A poor woman's sacrifice consisted of a pair of birds. The traders at the Temple sold these in wicker baskets at outrageous prices. The situation grew so bad that the rabbi Simon ben-Gamaliel put a controlled price on them. The birds were killed and plucked before being offered on the altar.

The priesthood

There were thousands of priests. They performed the ritual acts of Judaism such as sacrificing and offering incense. These acts were forbidden to ordinary Jews. The priests were also the religious authorities with responsibility for interpreting the Mosaic law. Priests had to be free from physical defects and descended from Aaron. Although priests and the rest of the Temple staff were drawn from the tribe of Levi they were known separately as priests and levites. They lived on a tax (tithe) paid by the rest of the people.

LEFT: the simple garb of the ordinary priest. It consisted of white linen underpants, a long white linen close-fitting tunic with a long girdle and a hat also made of white linen.

LEFT: an incense shovel from En Gedi. Burning coals were placed on the shovel and incense was kept in the two small dishes on either side. When needed it was sprinkled on the burning coals.

ABOVE: the elaborate dress of the high priest. He wore the same clothes as the ordinary priest covered by a blue robe fringed with gold bells and pomegranates. Over these he wore a short cloak embroidered with gold, red, blue and purple. He wore a gold purse encrusted with jewels on his chest. His head-dress was swathed in blue.

The high priest

High priests were descendants of Zadok the first high priest. After the return from Babylon the high priest became head of state. This double title was usurped by the Hasmonaeans who were not descended from Zadok.

Under Herod and the Romans the high priest was nominated and sacked by the king or Roman governor and became their puppet. There were 28 high priests between 37 BC and 70 AD. The high priests' families formed an aristocracy known as the chief priests. The high priest only officiated on Sabbaths, new moons and national festivals.

The priests' vestments

The ordinary priests wore white underpants covered by a long white gown tied with a girdle, and a white hat.

The high priest wore the same garments but over the white gown he wore a blue robe hanging down to his feet. At the bottom it had tassels with alternate golden bells and pomegranates hanging from them. Over this he wore a cape (ephod) embroidered in bands of gold, purple, scarlet and blue. He wore a gold purse inset with 12 precious stones on his chest. This was attached to two gold brooches inset with sardonyxes on his shoulders.

The day of a priest

Priests rose before dawn, took a ritual bath and then dressed. In the Chamber of Hewn Stone they drew lots for their duties – offering sacrifice, cleaning the altar, lighting the lamps, etc. At dawn a spotless ewe-lamb was killed. It was cut up on the marble tables to the right of the altar and portions of the lamb were burned.

All the priests and levites were called to the morning service by the clash of a gong being thrown on to the pavement in front of the Temple. The ceremony which was accompanied by music and singing lasted several hours.

The rest of the morning was spent in the offering of private sacrifices. As evening approached a second communal sacrifice was offered and more prayers recited. During the night the Temple and its courts were guarded by priests and levites. A priest was also left to keep the fire burning at the altar.

The death of Miriam

Herod returned to Judea in a state of great exhilaration and rushed to tell his beloved Miriam of his good fortune. She met him with a hail of abuse. Miriam had found out about his orders for her death. He tried to explain. He protested his love, but it was all in vain. His sister Salome and his mother Cyprus did everything they could to make matters worse. In his depression Herod willingly listened to their lies.

Meanwhile Octavian was heading for Egypt. Cleopatra was still holding on, hoping for a change of fortune. Herod, looking for an excuse to get away from problems at home, went to join his new patron. Octavian rewarded his devotion by giving him back the territories Cleopatra had taken from him. But he went further than this and added Samaria and the coastal strip to Herod's realm. He also made him a present of Cleopatra's 400 strong bodyguard of Gauls.

Herod's political success contrasted badly with his family problems. Miriam's love had turned to hatred. She was sure that Herod was infatuated with her and could never harm her, so she tormented him unmercifully. She scorned his sister and his mother for their low birth. For a year Herod suffered constant abuse. Then, egged on by Salome and Cyprus who devised an elaborate plot against Miriam, he charged her with adultery. She was found guilty and executed.

Herod suffered terrible remorse over the death of Miriam. He began to drink heavily and soon afterwards fell ill. During his illness Alexandra tried to sieze control of Jerusalem. Her plot failed and Herod, who no longer had to consider Miriam's feelings, gave orders for Alexandra's execution. These events brutalised Herod. From this point his rule became more oppressive.

Alexandra was the last of the Hasmonaeans. Herod ordered a purge of their supporters and over the next few months many of them, including several of his own friends, went to the gallows. But as usual repression only gave birth to further plots. Ten conspirators who planned to assassinate Herod in the theatre for his 'unJewish activities' were betrayed and executed. But most trouble makers simply disappeared into Hyrcania in the Judean wilderness. The fortress gained a sinister reputation as many a critic was dragged there never to be seen again.

ABOVE: 1 One of the jars containing the Dead Sea scrolls
2 A fragment of one of the scrolls
3 A clay inkwell
4 A reed pen

ABOVE: one of the writing tables and a bench found in the scriptorium or writing room, of the Essene community at Qumran near the Dead Sea.

RIGHT: a writing palette found in the scriptorium at Qumran.

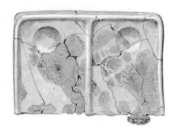

The Sadducees

During the 2nd century BC Judaism split into two factions, the Sadducees and the Pharisees. The Sadducees were an aristocratic party made up of the priests and levites plus the rich landowners, courtiers and merchants.

The Sadducees accepted the law of Moses literally. They rejected anything not found there. They believed that Jahweh was not concerned with everyday life and that the individual must solve his own problems. They rejected such teachings as the resurrection of the dead, the immortality of the soul and the Messiah.

The Scribes and Pharisees

The Scribes originally arranged and copied the scriptures. This responsible task made them the chief authorities on the subject. By the period we are dealing with they had become almost identical with the Pharisees. The Pharisees were a middle class group who believed that the law of Moses was a living code that needed constant interpretation. Their teachings formed a guide to the law which they believed was inspired. They believed in the immortality of the soul, the resurrection of the dead and in demons and angels.

The Pharisees formed their own communities either in special villages or in confined areas of towns.

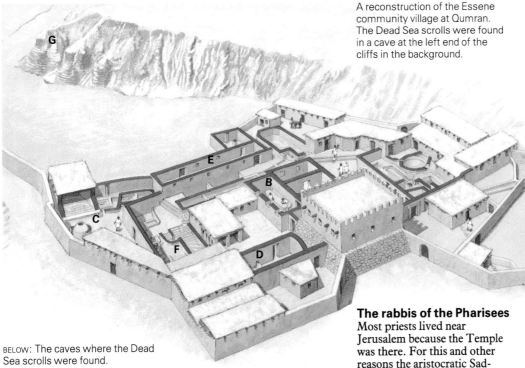

A reconstruction of the Essene community village at Qumran. The Dead Sea scrolls were found in a cave at the left end of the cliffs in the background.

A The aqueduct bringing in water from the hills. It ran right through the village filling several cisterns and ritual baths.
B The scriptorium
C Potter's kiln
D Kitchens
E The assembly hall and refectory
F The laundry
G The scroll caves

BELOW: The caves where the Dead Sea scrolls were found.

BELOW: 'monks' working in the scriptorium at Qumran.

The rabbis of the Pharisees

Most priests lived near Jerusalem because the Temple was there. For this and other reasons the aristocratic Sadducees had lost touch with the common country people who turned to Pharisees for advice. Their rabbis were the teachers of the law. They were not professional teachers and often did menial jobs.

These rabbis sometimes interpreted the law so strictly that at times it became almost meaningless. There is a famous tract where they actually debated whether or not it was right to eat an egg that had been laid on the Sabbath day.

They made the rules on purity into an intricate code. They insisted on strict personal hygiene. Food had to be cleansed and eaten off cleansed plates with cleansed hands. They would not eat in the houses of those they considered to be sinners in order to avoid contamination.

The Sanhedrin

The Sanhedrin was the supreme council and court of the Jews. It decided the meaning of the Mosaic law. It was dominated by the Sadducees. It had opposed Herod and when he became king he executed 45 of its 71 members and reduced it to a purely religious council. The members of the council sat in a semi-circle with three rows of disciples behind them. The president sat in the centre with the elders on either side. The decisions were noted by two clerks who stood in front of them.

The Essenes

In the summer of 1947 a Bedouin boy who had lost one of his goats climbed up a cliff overlooking the Dead Sea and stumbled into a cave full of scrolls. These were the famous Dead Sea scrolls, the library of a religious community that had lived there 2,000 years before. These people were Essenes, an extreme sect of the Pharisees. They disapproved of religious practices at Jerusalem and had withdrawn to the wilderness. Their religious leader, possibly called the Teacher of Righteousness, may have been executed, possibly crucified. The practices of the Essenes bear a remarkable similarity to those of early Christianity. They lived a communal life and shared their possessions. Their communal meals seem to foreshadow Christian communion. They practised baptism and believed that the end of the world was imminent.

There were Essene communities in Judea and Galilee.

There can be little doubt that they had an influence on both John the Baptist and Jesus of Nazareth.

The Messiah

For centuries many Jews had believed that a deliverer (Messiah) would lead them to victory over their enemies. He would be a descendant of David. The Essenes appear to have expected two Messiahs, a king Messiah from the house of David and a priest Messiah. The Sadducees ridiculed the whole idea of the Messiah.

The other side of the coin

Even before the fall of Antony, Judea was beginning to flourish. When Octavian, who now became the emperor Augustus, extended Herod's realm the king embarked on an ambitious building programme. Two cities were built to govern the newly acquired territories. In Samaria the old city of the same name was enlarged and renamed Sebaste, the Greek for Augustus. It was a gentile city and its citadel was crowned by a temple to Augustus. A military colony was set up there and it seems that Herod considered ruling from Sebaste in order to escape the restrictions of Jerusalem. He was a gentile at heart and pined for their more relaxed and liberal way of life. He tried to encourage fashionable Greek culture in Judea, and even built a theatre and amphitheatre in Jerusalem. But he constantly came up against objections from the strict Jews who saw any outside influences as a threat to their culture and religion.

Some two years after Herod had begun to rebuild Samaria, Judea was struck by famine and plague. The crops failed and the cattle died. Many interpreted the disaster as God's punishment on Herod for his gentile sympathies. But the king, in a genuine act of compassion for his subjects, converted all the gold and silver ornaments in his palaces into coinage and bought food from Egypt to feed his people.

Once the famine was over Herod was able to devote his energies to his building programme. Besides Samaria itself, a town named Antipatris after his father was founded in western Samaria, and a military colony, Gaba, was established in the valley of Jezreel, on the borders of Samaria and Galilee, to discourage outbreaks of violence between the two areas.

The most famous of Herod's new towns was the port of Caesarea. This was begun in 22 BC and took twelve years to complete. It had a great semi-circular artificial harbour. The city contained a theatre, an amphitheatre and a temple to Augustus, raised on a high platform overlooking the harbour. Caesarea was essentially a gentile city like the others along the coast. It was close to the province of Syria making it very convenient as an embarkation point.

There was a Jewish community in Caesarea. They occupied the northern end of the city where the earlier town of Strato's Tower had stood. The foundations of a synagogue have been found there. It seems certain that Herod intended to move his seat of government here. It had all the amenities the king loved so much.

ABOVE: the remains of the aqueduct built by Herod to bring water into the city from the hills in the north-east.

LEFT: an aerial view of the harbour at Caesarea. Herod's quays can be seen dark beneath the sea. The east (right) side of the harbour has filled up with sand.

BELOW: a reconstruction of the port of Caesarea. Archaeologists have discovered much of the street plan of the city and the line of the walls. The general shape of the harbour is also known.
1 The theatre 2 The temple of Augustus 3 The amphitheatre
4 The aqueduct

The new port at Caesarea

Caesarea was Herod's window on the Graeco-Roman world he loved. It was a gentile city but had a small Jewish quarter. It was named in honour of the emperor Augustus Caesar. A temple dedicated to the emperor was built in a prominent position overlooking the harbour. There had been no good harbour on the Jewish coast and Herod hoped that his new port would capture the trade with the east.

Caesarea contained all the modern amenities – theatre, amphitheatre, stadium and public baths. The public buildings, including Herod's palace, were built of white marble which had to be imported. The palace later became the seat of the Roman governor.

The city also had an elaborate sewerage system. The sewers were designed so that they were cleansed by the sea when the wind blew from the west.

A modern harbour 2,000 years old

The vast artificial harbour was about 500m long and 270m wide. It had broad quays defended by walls and towers. Within the walls were vaulted rooms used as living quarters by the sailors. The harbour entrance faced north protecting it from the prevailing southwest wind.

Herod's great harbour has disappeared beneath the waves but its remains can clearly be seen from the air. In recent years divers have examined the old quays. They have also discovered the base of a huge tower which guarded the harbour entrance and may have served as a light-house.

The most amazing discovery was made in 1982 when the remains of a number of wooden frames were found. Concrete had been poured into these and left to set under water – a modern technique.

The rebuilding of the Temple

Since the murder of Aristobulus some 15 years earlier Herod had kept complete control over the office of high priest and locked up the sacred garments in the Antonia fortress. After the death of Aristobulus, Hananel had been reappointed as high priest but he had in time been replaced by Jesus son of Phiabi.

After the death of Miriam we hear nothing of Herod's love life for about four years but he could never resist a pretty face. Stories reached his ears of another Miriam – the most beautiful woman of her time. The combintaion of beauty and that fateful name can hardly have failed to excite Herod. At first sight he fell in love again. Miriam's father was an insignificant priest named Simon. Herod knew that he could not marry into such a family without sacrificing his dignity. But his passion was not to be thwarted. He sacked the high priest Jesus and appointed Simon. He could hardly do better than marry the high priest's daughter.

The first Miriam had borne Herod two sons, Alexander and Aristobulus. Perhaps because of his new marriage he now sent them to Rome to be educated and the emperor Augustus took them into his own home. About this time trouble broke out in the area to the north-east of the Sea of Galilee and Augustus placed the area under Herod's rule.

Herod did not restrict his building programme to his newly acquired territories nor even to his own realm. He paid for the erection of public buildings all over the east. In Jerusalem he began two projects. The first was the building of a large palace complex in the upper city of Jerusalem. The second was the project for which he would always be remembered: the rebuilding of the Temple. His plans for it were on such a magnificent scale that, in spite of their enthusiasm for the project, the people doubted that he would ever complete it. In fact what they feared most was that he would destroy the existing Temple and not be able to afford to complete the new one. They refused to agree to the rebuilding until all the materials and workmen had been assembled.

The Temple had been rebuilt by Zerubbabel after the Jews returned from exile in Babylon. It had been a poor replacement for Solomon's magnificent sanctuary. Herod was determined that his Temple would outshine Solomon's in all its glory. The vast artificial platform on which he constructed it remains to this day and is he most dominant feature of Jerusalem.

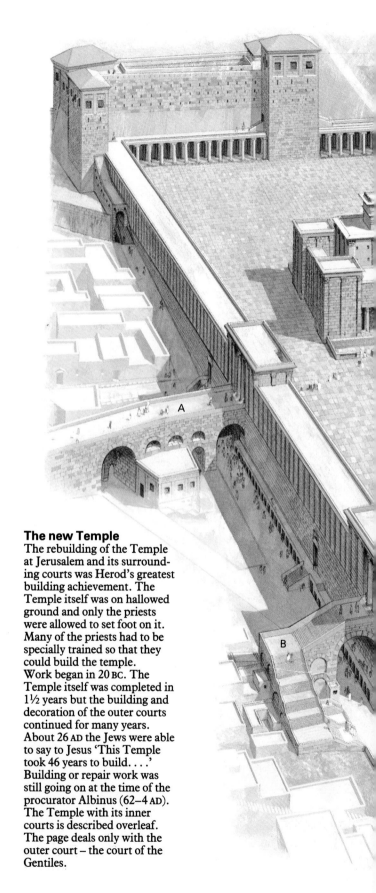

The new Temple
The rebuilding of the Temple at Jerusalem and its surrounding courts was Herod's greatest building achievement. The Temple itself was on hallowed ground and only the priests were allowed to set foot on it. Many of the priests had to be specially trained so that they could build the temple.
Work began in 20 BC. The Temple itself was completed in 1½ years but the building and decoration of the outer courts continued for many years. About 26 AD the Jews were able to say to Jesus 'This Temple took 46 years to build....' Building or repair work was still going on at the time of the procurator Albinus (62–4 AD). The Temple with its inner courts is described overleaf. The page deals only with the outer court – the court of the Gentiles.

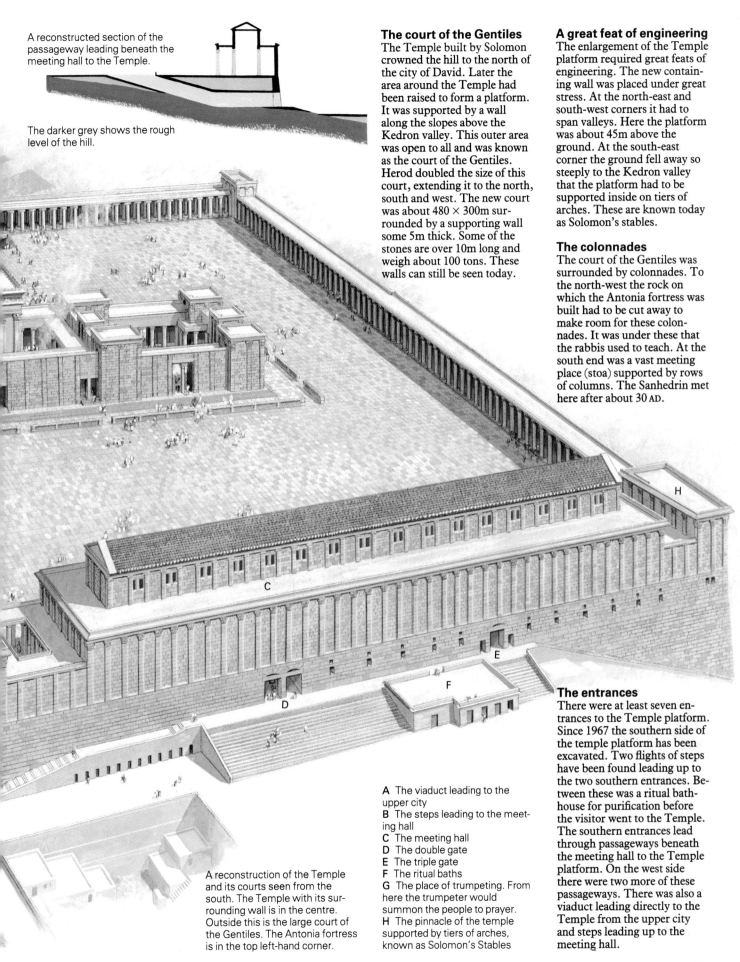

A reconstructed section of the passageway leading beneath the meeting hall to the Temple.

The darker grey shows the rough level of the hill.

The court of the Gentiles

The Temple built by Solomon crowned the hill to the north of the city of David. Later the area around the Temple had been raised to form a platform. It was supported by a wall along the slopes above the Kedron valley. This outer area was open to all and was known as the court of the Gentiles. Herod doubled the size of this court, extending it to the north, south and west. The new court was about 480 × 300m surrounded by a supporting wall some 5m thick. Some of the stones are over 10m long and weigh about 100 tons. These walls can still be seen today.

A great feat of engineering

The enlargement of the Temple platform required great feats of engineering. The new containing wall was placed under great stress. At the north-east and south-west corners it had to span valleys. Here the platform was about 45m above the ground. At the south-east corner the ground fell away so steeply to the Kedron valley that the platform had to be supported inside on tiers of arches. These are known today as Solomon's stables.

The colonnades

The court of the Gentiles was surrounded by colonnades. To the north-west the rock on which the Antonia fortress was built had to be cut away to make room for these colonnades. It was under these that the rabbis used to teach. At the south end was a vast meeting place (stoa) supported by rows of columns. The Sanhedrin met here after about 30 AD.

A reconstruction of the Temple and its courts seen from the south. The Temple with its surrounding wall is in the centre. Outside this is the large court of the Gentiles. The Antonia fortress is in the top left-hand corner.

A The viaduct leading to the upper city
B The steps leading to the meeting hall
C The meeting hall
D The double gate
E The triple gate
F The ritual baths
G The place of trumpeting. From here the trumpeter would summon the people to prayer.
H The pinnacle of the temple supported by tiers of arches, known as Solomon's Stables

The entrances

There were at least seven entrances to the Temple platform. Since 1967 the southern side of the temple platform has been excavated. Two flights of steps have been found leading up to the two southern entrances. Between these was a ritual bath-house for purification before the visitor went to the Temple. The southern entrances lead through passageways beneath the meeting hall to the Temple platform. On the west side there were two more of these passageways. There was also a viaduct leading directly to the Temple from the upper city and steps leading up to the meeting hall.

The return of Alexander and Aristobulus

The Temple itself was completed in a year and a half. So that the area would not be defiled, 1000 priests had had to be trained as masons. Although the new Temple conformed with all the requirements of Jewish law Herod could not resist his impulse to place a statue – a large golden eagle – above the main gate. Many Jews were horrified by the statue as their religion forbids the making of 'graven images'. When the Temple was finished Herod sacrificed 300 oxen to Jahweh. Work on the outer courts of the Temple went on for many years after Herod's death.

When the Temple had been dedicated, Herod decided to visit Rome to see his two sons and pay his respects to the emperor. Augustus had formed an attachment to the two boys and agreed to let Herod choose his own successor. The two princes had completed their education. Herod brought them home to Jerusalem and arranged marriages for them. For several years he had enjoyed domestic peace but with the return of the princes came all the old family jealousies.

Herod's sister Salome realised that if the two boys ever came to power they would try to avenge their mother's death. The palace intrigues began again. By subtle innuendo and half-truths Salome, supported by Herod's brother Pheroras, gradually managed to turn him against the boys. These two never ceased to undermine the position of the princes who, like their mother, responded with hatred for their father and his family. At first Herod had tried to ignore the slanders but at last his brother and sister got through to him. Herod had always intended that Alexander and Aristobulus should succeed him and they knew this. More than twenty years earlier when Miriam had first been betrothed to him he had sent away his first wife Doris and her son Antipater. He now recalled them. He wanted to warn the two princes that whilst Antipater lived their succession was by no means certain. This only made matters worse. Antipater, joined Salome in her campaign against the youths. He was far more subtle than his aunt. He employed people to spread malicious rumours about his half-brothers and then, rather unconvincingly, defended the two boys before their father. Herod warmed to his elder son for his unselfish defence of the princes. He wrote a letter to Rome praising Antipater who soon became accepted as Herod's successor.

Antipater's and Salome's campaign against the princes was so successful that Herod began to hate and fear the youths. In desperation he decided to ask the advice of the emperor Augustus. He took them to Italy and accused them of plotting to assassinate him and seize the throne. Augustus knew the two princes well and was unconvinced by Herod's charges. He reprimanded the princes for not paying proper respect to their father and managed to reconcile them.

On his return from Italy Herod addressed the people on the Temple platform, telling them what had happened. He then publicly named his successors – first Antipater and then Alexander and Aristobulus.

Caesarea was completed in 10 BC. The king inaugurated the new city with lavish games. These festivities must also have celebrated the new concord that he believed he had found within his family. But it was not to be.

One of the notices warning non-Jews not to enter the inner courts of the Temple. This was discovered in 1871. The translated Greek inscription reads 'No foreigner is to enter within the balustrade and enclosure around the Temple area. Whoever is caught will have himself to blame for his death which will follow.'

The Temple of Jahweh
There are no visible remains of the Temple itself. No excavations have been carried out on the site of the inner courts nor on that of the Temple itself. Our only guide is the ancient writings which unfortunately contradict each other. Josephus gives a full account of the Temple. He was a priest and most scholars accept his account.
The easiest way to describe the Temple and its courts is to take an imaginary walk with a Jewish family through them. After crossing the court of the Gentiles we come to a low wall with notices on it in Greek and Latin stating that any non-Jew found beyond this point will be executed.

A representation of the seven-pronged lampstand (menorah) scratched on the wall of a house excavated in the old Jewish quarter of Jerusalem.

The Temple 2

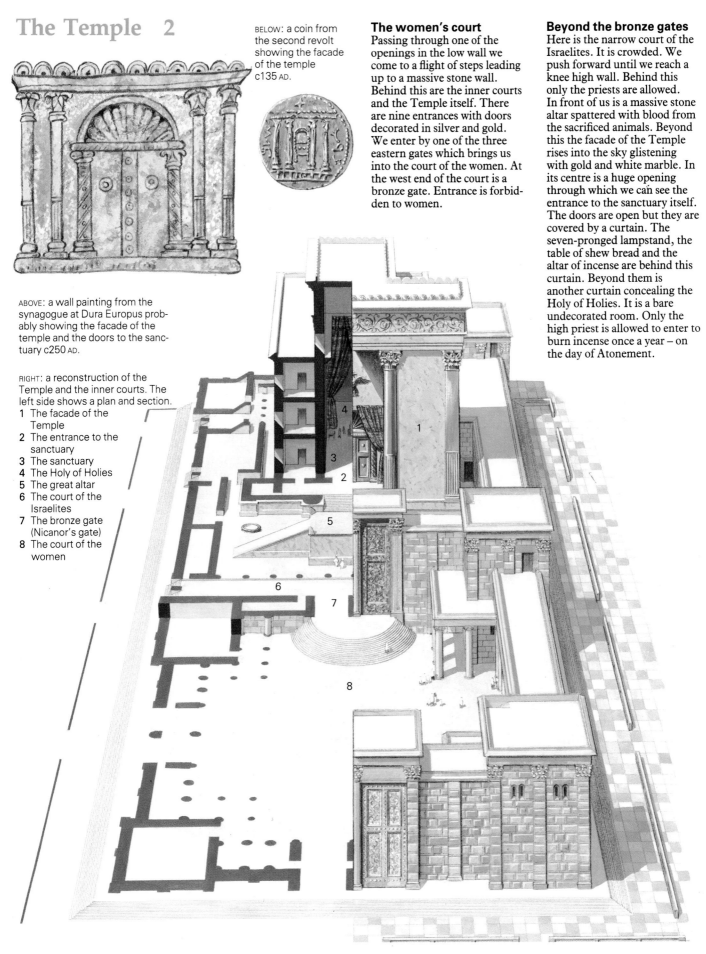

BELOW: a coin from the second revolt showing the facade of the temple c135 AD.

ABOVE: a wall painting from the synagogue at Dura Europus probably showing the facade of the temple and the doors to the sanctuary c250 AD.

RIGHT: a reconstruction of the Temple and the inner courts. The left side shows a plan and section.

1 The facade of the Temple
2 The entrance to the sanctuary
3 The sanctuary
4 The Holy of Holies
5 The great altar
6 The court of the Israelites
7 The bronze gate (Nicanor's gate)
8 The court of the women

The women's court

Passing through one of the openings in the low wall we come to a flight of steps leading up to a massive stone wall. Behind this are the inner courts and the Temple itself. There are nine entrances with doors decorated in silver and gold. We enter by one of the three eastern gates which brings us into the court of the women. At the west end of the court is a bronze gate. Entrance is forbidden to women.

Beyond the bronze gates

Here is the narrow court of the Israelites. It is crowded. We push forward until we reach a knee high wall. Behind this only the priests are allowed. In front of us is a massive stone altar spattered with blood from the sacrificed animals. Beyond this the facade of the Temple rises into the sky glistening with gold and white marble. In its centre is a huge opening through which we can see the entrance to the sanctuary itself. The doors are open but they are covered by a curtain. The seven-pronged lampstand, the table of shew bread and the altar of incense are behind this curtain. Beyond them is another curtain concealing the Holy of Holies. It is a bare undecorated room. Only the high priest is allowed to enter to burn incense once a year – on the day of Atonement.

More wives – more problems

Age had not muted Herod's passion for a pretty face. When his love for the beautiful Miriam II waned he married again ... and again ... and again. As each new wife joined the harem she took sides in the domestic quarrels. In spite of the bedlam this caused, Herod continued to marry, perhaps in the hope that he might one day find a wife who actually liked him. In the end he had no fewer than nine wives bickering around the palace. From these he produced an interminable string of children.

Matters were further confused by attempts to marry some of the children off within the confines of his own family. Aristobulus had been married to Salome's daughter. But Salome out of hatred for Miriam's sons persuaded her daughter to refuse Aristobulus his marital rights. Herod had earmarked one of his own daughters for his brother, but Pheroras insulted the king by rejecting his offer as he wanted to marry a slave girl. This caused a split between them.

Pheroras then accused the king of 'fancying' Alexander's young wife Glaphyra. The young Alexander responded with a stream of abuse against his father. The whole thing blew up with Herod accusing Pheroras and Pheroras blaming it all on the arch-intriguer Salome.

Incredible though it may seem the ageing Salome now fell in love. The unlucky man was Syllaeus, prime minister of Herod's old enemies the Nabataean Arabs. Herod was horrified when he found out about the affair. He was even more appalled when Syllaeus asked for his sister's hand in marriage. Herod told him that he would have to be circumcised and embrace the Jewish faith. This was too much for Syllaeus and he returned to his own country.

Herod, ever sensuous, had some rather pretty eunuchs who attended to his personal needs. He was very fond of these effeminate creatures. Rumour was spread that Alexander had become sexually involved with them. Herod had them tortured on the rack and Antipater managed to get them to incriminate Alexander. Herod's anger approached madness and he began to purge his court of all those of uncertain loyalty. To save their own lives his courtiers began to accuse each other and many a head rolled. Herod soon recovered and realised what was happening. He felt remorse for the innocent people he had executed but in his usual bull-headed fashion he made amends by executing the informers as well.

Antipater succeeded in blackening the names of Alexander and Aristobulus. Herod was convinced that they were plotting against him. Alexander's friends were tortured. When they went to their deaths with nothing to tell, Antipater pretended to show admiration for their loyalty to the prince, turning even lack of evidence to his advantage. Finally Antipater's efforts paid off and the outline of a plot began to emerge. It was alleged that Alexander was planning a hunting accident for his father. A forged letter from Alexander to Aristobulus was produced to support the allegation. Herod believed the forged evidence and arrested Alexander. Blinded by his hatred for his father's family Alexander admitted the charges and got his revenge by claiming that Pheroras and Salome had been involved in the plot.

In the midst of the confusion Alexander's father-in-law, the king of Cappadocia, came to Judea in fear for his daughter's life. The wily old Cappadoian, by pouring abuse on Alexander managed to get Herod to defend his son. He then diverted suspicion on to Pheroras. Herod was at odds with his brother anyway and willingly made him the scapegoat. So once more the two princes were reprieved.

As if Herod's domestic problems were not enough, he now began to make political mistakes. By refusing Syllaeus permission to marry Salome he had made an inveterate enemy. Syllaeus began to support Herod's enemies in Trachonitis to the east of the Sea of Galilee. Trachonitis had been given to Herod by Augustus. A guerrilla war developed of the type so familiar to the modern world. Herod was unable to capture the rebels as they sought refuge in Arabia. In retaliation the king massacred their kinsmen in Trachonitis. This of course made matters worse and the attacks increased.

Herod waited until Syllaeus was out of the country. Then with the consent of the governor of Syria he made a raid into Arabia and ran the guerrillas to ground. Having destroyed them in their stronghold he withdrew to his own kingdom.

Syllaeus happened to be in Rome at the time and he complained to Augustus, grossly exaggerating the scale of Herod's raid. The emperor reacted angrily. He did not query the details. He only enquired whether the story was true. He then wrote a harsh letter to Herod reducing him from the position of friend to that of subject. Herod's world seemed to be collapsing around him. He sent embassies to Rome but these were sent back unheard.

The Herodian dynasty

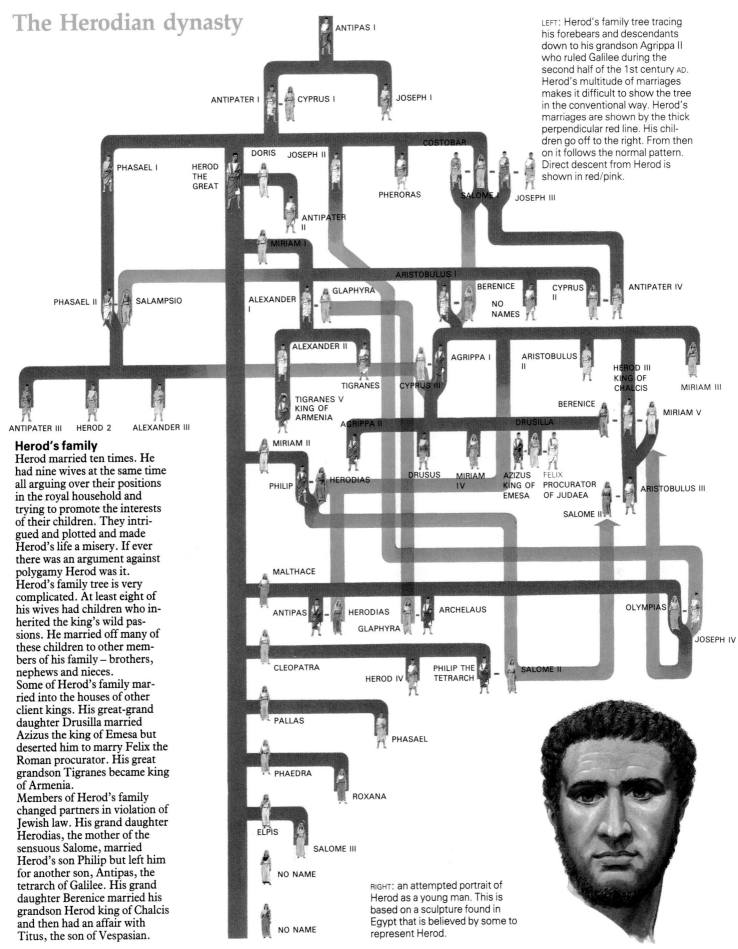

ANTIPAS I

ANTIPATER I – CYPRUS I   JOSEPH I

PHASAEL I   HEROD THE GREAT   DORIS   JOSEPH II   COSTOBAR

PHERORAS   SALOME I   JOSEPH III

ANTIPATER II

MIRIAM I

PHASAEL II – SALAMPSIO   ALEXANDER I   GLAPHYRA   ARISTOBULUS I   BERENICE NO NAMES   CYPRUS II   ANTIPATER IV

ALEXANDER II   AGRIPPA I   ARISTOBULUS II   HEROD III KING OF CHALCIS   MIRIAM III

TIGRANES   CYPRUS III

ANTIPATER III   HEROD 2   ALEXANDER III   TIGRANES V KING OF ARMENIA   BERENICE   MIRIAM V

AGRIPPA II   DRUSILLA   ARISTOBULUS III

MIRIAM II   DRUSUS   MIRIAM IV   AZIZUS KING OF EMESA   FELIX PROCURATOR OF JUDAEA

PHILIP – HERODIAS   SALOME II

MALTHACE

ANTIPAS – HERODIAS   ARCHELAUS   OLYMPIAS

GLAPHYRA   JOSEPH IV

CLEOPATRA   HEROD IV   PHILIP THE TETRARCH – SALOME II

PALLAS   PHASAEL

PHAEDRA   ROXANA

ELPIS   SALOME III

NO NAME

NO NAME

Herod's family

Herod married ten times. He had nine wives at the same time all arguing over their positions in the royal household and trying to promote the interests of their children. They intrigued and plotted and made Herod's life a misery. If ever there was an argument against polygamy Herod was it.

Herod's family tree is very complicated. At least eight of his wives had children who inherited the king's wild passions. He married off many of these children to other members of his family – brothers, nephews and nieces.

Some of Herod's family married into the houses of other client kings. His great-grand daughter Drusilla married Azizus the king of Emesa but deserted him to marry Felix the Roman procurator. His great grandson Tigranes became king of Armenia.

Members of Herod's family changed partners in violation of Jewish law. His grand daughter Herodias, the mother of the sensuous Salome, married Herod's son Philip but left him for another son, Antipas, the tetrarch of Galilee. His grand daughter Berenice married his grandson Herod king of Chalcis and then had an affair with Titus, the son of Vespasian.

RIGHT: an attempted portrait of Herod as a young man. This is based on a sculpture found in Egypt that is believed by some to represent Herod.

The end of Alexander and Aristobulus

Alexander and Aristobulus were now implicated in a new plot against their father. Once more Salome urged her brother to punish them and this time she got her way. Herod wrote to Augustus laying the evidence before him.

The emperor had by now realised that he had acted over-hastily in condemning Herod for his Arabian venture. Nonetheless he must have been fed up to the teeth with Herod's domestic problems. He advised Herod to convene a court at the Roman colony of Beirut, and bring the princes to trial before the governor of Syria, and whoever else he considered fitting. When assembled the court consisted of 150 members. Herod accused his sons before the gathering. He did not allow them to appear at the court or to offer a defence. Nor did he allow the evidence to be examined. In spite of a plea for leniency by the governor of Syria, the other members of the court who were of Herod's choice returned the guilty verdict Herod wanted.

The king returned to Caesarea where he had to face trouble from his soldiers who had liked the princes. Three hundred of the soldiers were arrested and beaten to death by the crowd on Herod's orders. Aristobulus and Alexander were then taken to Sebaste, where Herod had married their mother, and there strangled. At night their bodies were removed to Alexandrium where most of the Hasmonaeans had been buried.

All this time Pheroras had remained true to his slave girl and in spite of Herod's constant threats refused to give her up. In exasperation Herod banished him from court, sending him to govern Peraea. Several years earlier the king had persuaded Augustus to make his brother tetrarch of this area. Pheroras swore that he would not return until he heard of his brother's death.

The fall of Antipater

Antipater's succession now seemed secure and gradually Herod began to transfer power to him. But Antipater was not satisfied with this. He couldn't wait to be king and grumbled about Herod's seemingly never-ending life. Salome grew frightened of Antipater's increasing power and endeavoured to undermine his position. But Herod knew his sister all too well by this time and refused to believe her slanders. With complete confidence in him he sent Antipater on an embassy to Rome.

Before Antipater departed he had a secret meeting with Pheroras. The two of them hatched a plot to poison the king during Antipater's absence. However before the plot could be brought to fruition Pheroras died under suspicious circumstances. Pheroras's slaves were racked and under torture a whole web of palace intrigues were laid bare. As these seemed to support what Salome had been saying Herod could hardly doubt them.

The story of Antipater's plan to have his father poisoned in his absence was confirmed by Pheroras' slave wife. Herod was finally convinced when the poison itself was produced. It was also revealed that the beautiful Miriam II had been a party to the plot. This must have been a terrible affront to Herod's pride. He divorced her immediately, and sacked her father as high priest.

Herod was determined that Antipater should not escape. Although it was seven months before he returned, Herod's secret police were so efficient that not a word of the discovery of the plot reached his son. Antipater arrived at Caesarea and headed for Jerusalem where his father was entertaining the governor of Syria. Next day Antipater was put on trial before the governor. He tried to defend himself but the evidence was overwhelming. The governor gave no formal verdict but Herod had his son imprisoned and sent letters to Augustus telling him of the situation.

Worn out by the never ending intrigues Herod fell ill and seemed to be on the point of death. He revised his will leaving his kingdom to his youngest son Antipas.

Hearing that the king was dying, two of the leading rabbis who had long been scandalised by the great golden eagle that Herod had erected over the main gate of the Temple encouraged their students to tear it down. The young men climbed up on to the roof of the Temple, knocked down the statue and began hacking it to pieces. They were arrested and sent to Jericho. Here they were brought before Herod who was by now too ill to stand.

Herod's anger was probably aggravated by his illness. Although he dealt mildly with the majority of the students he sacked the high priest and ordered those who had been responsible for the disturbance to be burned alive. The date of this event is known, for Josephus records that there was an eclipse of the moon that night (13 March 4 BC).

Jericho

Jericho

Jericho is the oldest and the lowest town in the world. The earliest remains at Jericho go back more than 11,000 years. Its altitude is 250m below sea level. Its site is the only oasis in the lower Jordan valley. It has a very mild climate in the winter which made it a very popular winter resort for the wealthy citizens of Jerusalem. The Hasmonaeans and Herod built palaces along the banks of the Wadi Qelt to the south-west of the old town.

ABOVE: the oasis of Jericho seen from the Wadi Qelt to the south-west of the old town. The picture shows the sharp contrast between the desert and the sown. In Herod's time the fertile land extended to the hills in the foreground. The palaces of Herod and the Hasmonaeans were in the middle distance along the banks of the wadi.

LEFT ABOVE: the luxuriant vegetation of the oasis.

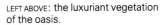

LEFT BELOW: the Wadi Qelt. The old road to Jerusalem passed this way. This is the setting of the good Samaritan story. The road was well known to the Galileans. To avoid going through Samaria they came down the Jordan valley as far as Jericho and then took this route to Jerusalem. Jesus of Nazareth went this way on his last journey to Jerusalem.

The end of Herod

Herod's death was now approaching and he was in great pain. He crossed the Jordan to bathe in the warm springs but this did not help so he returned to Jericho. On his death bed he received a letter from Augustus giving him permission to deal with Antipater as he saw fit. This pleased Herod but he did not give the order for Antipater's execution.

Meanwhile rumours spread that the king had died. Antipater heard them and his spirits rose. He offered his jailer a large bribe to release him. Herod was informed and issued the fatal order. Antipater's body was interred without ceremony in Hyrcania. Five days later the king died but not before he had once more changed his will. He divided his realm between three of his sons Antipas, Archelaus and Philip.

Herod's reign had been a long one. It was 35 years since he had returned from Rome as king. It is very difficult to assess the value of his reign for the Jews and gentiles saw him in very different lights. Although he was always careful to obey the Jewish law while in Judea he was at heart a gentile and the orthodox Jews could never forgive him for this.

His reign gave them a third of a century of peace and prosperity and the new harbour at Caesarea increased trade. But Herod's lavish building programmes cost immense sums of money and taxes were necessarily high. By the standards of the time he was not a bad ruler. He was brutal but far less so than the Hasmonaeans. Herod's greatest asset was in fact the very thing for which Jews most criticised him – his half-hearted attitude towards Judaism. Augustus had realised Herod's true value when he gave him Samaria and the coastal strip for although Herod was careful not to offend the Jews he did not oppress the Samaritans and non-Jews. A Hasmonaean ruler would certainly have persecuted them and similarly a non-Jewish ruler would have had little sympathy with the Jews.

Herod's greatest fault was his ungovernable passion both in love and hate. This coupled with his constant fear of losing his throne led to most of his 'crimes' especially those committed within his own family.

The crime for which today Herod is most notorious is of this type. This was the massacre of the little children recorded in the Gospel of Matthew. The historian Josephus, who was of Hasmonaean descent, takes great delight in cataloguing Herod's crimes. Yet he does not mention this. This is extraordinary for if it happened it must surely have been regarded as the worst of the king's atrocities. This omission by Josephus places it in the realm of belief rather than history. True or not the crime was certainly in character and reflects the bitter memory that the Jews had of Herod.

LEFT: the swimming bath excavated on the north side of the Wadi Qelt near Jericho. This is possibly where the young high priest Aristobulus was 'accidentally' drowned on Herod's orders. It is a double bath separated by a low wall on which the bathers could rest. The low mound to the right behind the swimming bath is the ruins of the Hasmonaean palace. In the time of the Herods a massive earth-filled plinth 6–7m high was built over the Hasmonaean building and another palace raised on top of it.
On the summit of the high hill, to the left of centre, Herod built a fortress defending the road to Jerusalem which ran to the right of it. He named the fortress Cyprus after his mother.

Herod's palace at Jericho

BELOW: the north wing of Herod's winter palace on the banks of the Wadi Qelt near Jericho.

1 The great columned reception hall. This is believed to be similar to the one in the palace at Jerusalem.

2 and **3** The colonnaded courts

4–7 The bathing rooms

4 Changing room (Apodyterium)

5 Warm rooms (Tepidaria)

6 Hot room (Caldarium) **7** Cold bath room (Frigidarium) **8** Service area

Herod's winter palace

About 250m to the east of the Hasmonaean palace archaeologists have uncovered an extensive palace complex along both sides of the wadi. This is believed to be one of Herod's palaces probably built in the last ten years of his reign. It incorporated several earlier buildings. To the south of the wadi was an older palace and a sunken garden with a large pool next to it. The most modern part was on the north bank of the wadi. It was connected to the southern complex by a bridge. The northern wing consisted of a large reception hall, two colonnaded courts and a Graeco-Roman bath house. Only the foundations of these buildings remain but fragments of the wall decoration have been found and it is clear that this was a more luxurious palace than that at Masada.

The divided kingdom

Archelaus gave his father a magnificent funeral. The body was carried on a golden bier and laid to rest at Herodium. He then sacrificed in the Temple. Here he found the people excited at the old king's death and still seething with anger over the golden eagle affair. The passover was due. Crowds were pouring into the city. The atmosphere was charged. Fearing an uprising he sent out some of his troops to control the crowds. It was the spark that was needed. The angry crowds turned on the soldiers and stoned them to death. Archelaus reacted by calling out the rest of his army. In the ensuing massacre about 3,000 people were killed.

Archelaus had to have his position confirmed. Leaving the country in the hands of the governor of Syria he sailed for Rome. Here he found his position challenged by his brother Antipas, his aunt Salome and other members of his family. Augustus was forced to witness the squabbling and scandal-mongering that had plagued Herod's household.

Meanwhile there was another uprising which the governor of Syria put down. He left a legion at Jerusalem to keep peace and returned to Syria. At Pentecost crowds once again poured into Jerusalem. Many came prepared to try and throw out the Romans. They climbed up on to the Temple porticoes and pelted the Romans with missiles. Unable to reach them with their heavy javelins, the legionaries set fire to the porticoes and brought them crashing down. The legionaries then broke into the Temple treasury and looted it. They retreated to the upper palace where they were besieged by the angry mob.

The revolt spread. Soon the whole country was up in arms. News reached the governor of Syria who returned with two more legions. He overran Galilee which had joined the revolt, burning Sepphoris and selling the people into slavery. He then marched on Jerusalem burning the towns and villages as he went. Those besieging the palace fled. Two thousand of the rebels were captured and crucified. He then returned to Syria leaving one legion at Jerusalem.

Meanwhile an embassy from the Jews had gone to beg Augustus to dissolve the kingdom. They were followed by another of Herod's sons, Philip. Augustus was compelled to make a quick decision and confirmed Herod's last will. Archelaus received Judea, Samaria and Idumaea. Antipas was given Galilee and Peraea, whilst Philip received the north-eastern territories.

ABOVE: the base of the 'Tower of David', the Hippicus tower, one of the three huge towers that Herod built at the north-west end of his palace.

BELOW: Jerusalem seen from Mt. Scopus. The Mount of Olives is on the left. The Kedron valley is in the centre. The Temple platform now crowned by the golden Dome of the Rock is right of it.

RIGHT: Jerusalem seen from the south as it must have looked at the time of Herod's death.
1 Upper palace with its three massive towers 2 Lower palace 3 Hasmonaean palace 4 Theatre 5 Upper forum 6 Xystus 7 Temple platform 8 Antonia 9 Bethesda hill and pools. The pool of Israel is out of sight 10 Probable site of Calvary.

Herod's Jerusalem

When Herod died in 4 BC he left Jerusalem looking very different from the city he had captured 33 years earlier. It was dominated by the new Temple platform which occupied about one-sixth of the city.

Herod's palace in the upper city crowded the western skyline. Parts of its artificial platform and the lower levels of the great north-west towers that defended it have been found. Herod also built a smaller palace, a theatre and a stadium. Early in his reign he remodelled the Bira fortress to the north of the Temple and renamed it Antonia after his patron Antony. The two pools on the Bethesda hill had been replaced by the larger pool of Israel at the north-east corner of the Temple platform. This pool was formed by the supporting wall of the platform damming the valley. These vast building projects required changing the very street plan of the city.

Herod was the greatest builder Palestine had ever known. The city changed little after his death.

PONTIUS PILATE AND JESUS

The years of Archelaus

Augustus' last words to Archelaus as he left Rome were that if he proved himself a worthy successor to his father he would be made king. Archelaus proved to be an inept, unjust and cruel ruler. He had inherited all his father's vices but none of his virtues and he ruled with complete disregard for the feelings and well-being of his people. His first act on returning to Jerusalem was to sack the high priest, making him the scapegoat for the recent troubles. But he soon fell out with his new high priest and replaced him also.

When visiting Cappadocia Archelaus met the king's daughter Glaphyra. She had been married to his brother Alexander who had been executed by Herod. Archelaus fell in love with her. His passion was so great that he divorced his wife and insisted on marrying her. This provoked an outcry from his people for Glaphyra had borne his brother's children and marriage was thus in flagrant breach of Jewish law. Archelaus' passion was not to last for long for Glaphyra soon died. After ten years of Archelaus the Jews and Samaritans sent a delegation to Rome to complain. Augustus stripped Archelaus of his title and banished him. In 6 AD Judea was placed under direct Roman rule.

Archelaus' brothers ruled more successfully. Antipas had a split realm for Galilee and Peraea were separated by the lands of the Decapolis. He was very like his father in his method of government and in his love of luxury. He rebuilt Sepphoris which had been destroyed by the Romans during the troubles that followed his father's death. He changed his father's hostile policy towards the Nabataean Arabs and tried to secure the borders of Peraea by marrying into their royal family.

Philip received the smallest share of Herod's kingdom. His realm consisted of the area to the north and east of the sea of Galilee. Here the Syrians and Greeks outnumbered the Jewish population. Perhaps because of this Philip proved to be an exceptionally good ruler. Like his father he was a great builder and erected a capital city near the source of the Jordan which he named Caesarea Philippi. He lacked his father's ambition and his cruelty. Both Antipas and Philip had long and successful reigns spanning more than a third of a century.

The Temple platform crowded for the Passover. The men wear prayer shawls and phylacteries – little boxes containing Bible tracts. The old woman in the corner is carrying a basket of two pigeons, 'the poor man's sacrifice', which she bought under the porticoes. The Antonia fortress looms in the background. It had one very high tower from which the whole Temple area could be seen. The fortress was permanently garrisoned by Roman troops. At the great feasts the soldiers stood guard on the porticoes in case of a riot.

execute as he saw fit within the general guide lines laid down at Rome. He established his seat of government (praetorium) in Herod's palace at Caesarea.

Government from Rome

Archelaus' realm was now converted into a minor province. It was governed by a Roman prefect, but under the watchful eye of the governor of Syria. Quirinius was sent out as the new governor of Syria with orders to make a census of all property and to sell off the estates of Archelaus. There can be little doubt that this was the famous census mentioned in the Gospel of Luke in connection with the birth of Jesus.

The census was bitterly resented by the Jews but the high priest tried to persuade them to accept it. However not all would listen to his advice. Resistance to the census was led by a man known as Judas the Galilean and a Pharisee named Zadduk. The revolt made little headway but it laid the foundations of the Zealot movement which preached the forcible removal of the Romans. The high priest's failure to gain overall acceptance of the census cost him his job. Quirinius replaced him with Ananus (the Anas of the New Testament) who kept his position until 15 AD.

The Romans set up their headquarters at Caesarea. The first three prefects governed for only three years each and we know little of events during their administration. In 14 AD Augustus died and was succeeded by Tiberius who made Valerius Gratus prefect of Judea. He ruled for eleven years (15–26 AD). Gratus had great problems with the high priesthood. He sacked Ananus but his successor also proved unacceptable. He was replaced by Eleazar the son of Ananus. A year later he also was deposed but even then Gratus was not satisfied. Finally he nominated Caiaphas, the son-in-law of Ananus. Caiaphas managed to hold on to office for 18 years (18–36 AD).

The Romans followed Herod's system to control the high priest. They took custody of his vestments. These were kept in the Antonia fortress which was permanently garrisoned by a cohort of auxiliary soldiers. After each festival the vestments would be packed up and sealed by the high priest and treasurers of the Temple. They were then deposited with the tribune in command of the garrison. The day before the next festival the treasurers would go to the Antonia, to inspect the seal and collect the garments again.

In 26 AD Tiberius replaced Gratus with the notorious Pontius Pilate. And so one comes to those fateful years which were to have such a profound effect on the western world.

Provincial governors

There were two types of province – 'senatorial' and 'imperial'. Senatorial provinces were under the control of the senate which was similar to the British House of Lords. They were governed by former consuls and praetors. These were the highest Roman magistrates. Imperial provinces were under the control of the emperor. Governors of these provinces were nominated by the emperor. A governor could be either a senator with the title of legate, or be a non-senator with the title of prefect. Judea was an imperial province governed by a prefect.

Within his province the governor was supreme. The prefect of Judea had total authority over the provincials (peregrini). He could imprison, flog or

RIGHT: a reconstruction of the trial of Jesus of Nazareth set in Herod's palace in the upper city. The raised platform (tribunal) overlooks the great market place. From here the prefect could address the people and they could witness his justice. Pilate and his advisers are seated on the tribunal. In front of him are Jesus and his accusers. Witnesses wait in a side room.

BELOW: map showing the extent of the province and tetrarchies.

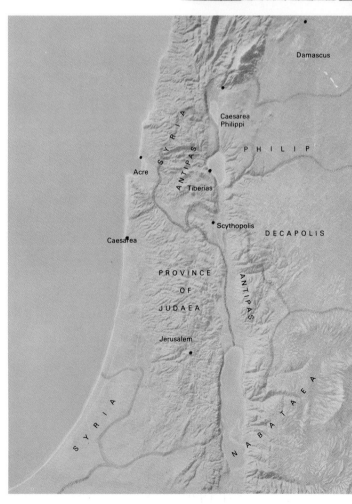

Damascus

Caesarea Philippi

S Y R I A

Acre

ANTIPAS

Tiberias

PHILIP

Scythopolis

DECAPOLIS

Caesarea

PROVINCE

OF

JUDAEA

ANTIPAS

Jerusalem

SYRIA

NABATAEA

The army
Archelaus had about 3,000 troops. These were taken over by the prefect and organised into six Roman auxiliary units. These were not legionaries. One was a cavalry unit – Ala I Sebastenorum and another an infantry unit – Cohors I Sebastenorum. These were originally from Samaria.

Taxation
Provinces had to pay tribute. The amount was estimated and the country split up into tax districts (toparchies). Rome had no civil service. Taxes were collected by private syndicates who made a profit by over-collecting. Tax collectors (publicani) were despised in the New Testament.
Taxes which were on goods were very high. When tithing and the Temple tax were added the burden was crippling.

Coinage
Many coins have been found from this period. Herod minted bronze coins but was forbidden to issue gold and silver money. He was careful not to offend his subjects and never put a human head or an animal on them. This practice was followed by the governors. However Pontius Pilate put Roman religious symbols on his coins which offended the Jews.

ABOVE: **1** Front and back of a coin of Herod the Great.
2 Front and back of a coin of Herod Antipas.

BELOW: a standard bearer with an image of the emperor. This scandalised the Jews.

ABOVE: **3** Front and back of a coin of Pontius Pilate with a lituus on it – a Roman religious symbol which was bound to upset the Jews.
4 Front and back of a coin of Tiberius. The coins are actual size.

The trial of Jesus of Nazareth
The prefect came up to Jerusalem for the main feasts. He would have made Herod's palace in the upper city his official residence It must have been here that the trial of Jesus of Nazareth took place.
The description of this trial fits what is known of provincial trials. There was no public prosecutor. Charges were brought by individuals: in this case the chief priests and elders. Witnesses were necessary and the accused had the right to cross examine them. The accused was given three opportunities to defend himself. If he refused he was found guilty. Roman trials were usually held in the open. The crowd of onlookers expressing their opinions was quite normal.

Pilate's reluctance
Pilate's reluctance to execute is puzzling. Jesus was accused of claiming to be the Messiah. Such a claim was tantamount to treason. Any prefect of Judea knew this. The Messiah was their constant nightmare. Their policy was to nip any potential uprising in the bud. One can only assume that Pilate disbelieved the priests and thought they were trying to involve him in a purely religious dispute.

An inscription set up by Pontius Pilate in which he refers to himself as (PRAEF)ECTUS – a prefect, not a procurator.

Jesus of Nazareth

Jesus was probably born in the last years of the reign of Herod the Great. He grew up at Nazareth, a village on the hills of Galilee overlooking the plain of Jezreel. (Nazareth is now a sprawling town). Since Jesus' childhood Galilee had been ruled by Antipas.

When Jesus was in his early twenties Antipas started building a magnificent new capital overlooking the western shore of the Sea of Galilee. He named the city Tiberias after the new emperor. However, old tombs were uncovered during building which rendered the site unclean in Jewish law. Antipas refused to abandon the city and was forced to people it with non-Jews.

This was not Antipas' only brush with Jewish law. Whilst visiting his half-brother Herod Philip (not to be confused with Philip the ruler of the realm to the north and east of the sea of Galilee) he met the beautiful Herodias, Herod the Great's granddaughter. She had married Herod Philip and borne him a daughter Salome. Antipas fell passionately in love with Herodias. He proposed marriage, and she accepted, on the condition that Antipas divorced his Arabian wife, daughter of the Nabataean king. Antipas' wife heard of the plan and fled to her father who broke off friendly relations with Antipas. The most outspoken of his critics was John the Baptist. He had been leading a religious revival in Peraea, Antipas' territory to the east of the Jordan. He had a great following amongst the ordinary people and Antipas feared an uprising. He had John arrested and imprisoned in the fortress of Machaerus where later he was beheaded. According to the gospels Antipas was frightened to execute John because of his popularity. They tell how Herodias' daughter Salome danced for Antipas who was so aroused that he promised her anything she desired. At Herodias' instigation Salome demanded John's head.

About the same time (between 26 and 33 AD) Jesus began his public life. He started preaching in Galilee making his headquarters at Capernaum on the north shore of the Sea of Galilee. His liberal teaching attracted great crowds but it also brought him into conflict with the Pharisees and Saducees. When he went up to Jerusalem for the Passover he was arrested and brought before the Sanhedrin. The following morning he was dragged before Pilate, charged with treason, and crucified.

Pontius Pilate

Pontius Pilate had arrived in Judea in 26 AD. He is described as greedy, vindictive and cruel. He should never have been prefect of Judea as he had nothing but contempt for Jewish customs. The governors before him had been careful not to offend the Jews. Pilate was deliberately provocative. The soldiers had been forbidden to carry their standards into Jerusalem because the images of the emperor on them offended against Jewish religious law. Pilate ordered his troops to take their standards into the city under the cover of darkness. The people found out what Pilate had done and an angry mob descended on Caesarea and besieged the prefect in his palace for five days. Only the timely removal of the standards prevented a more serious uprising and the massacre that would have followed.

Pilate's next mistake was unfortunate for he may have had the best of intentions. Jerusalem was always short of water and the governor decided to construct another aqueduct. His mistake was to pay for the building from the Temple treasury. The Jews of course were outraged. When next he visited Jerusalem Pilate was engulfed by a shrieking mob. He had expected this. Some of his soldiers dressed in Jewish costume had mingled with the crowd. On the agreed signal the disguised soldiers attacked the demonstrators with clubs and killed several of them. Other such acts of violence are hinted at in the New Testament.

It was customary for the prefect to move from Caesarea to Jerusalem with his forces for the main feasts as there was always the possibility of a disturbance when large numbers of people gathered in the city. During the feasts the Roman troops in the Antonia fortress descended on to the Temple porticoes to discourage trouble makers.

The prefects were not the only rulers who went up to Jerusalem for the feasts. Antipas and Philip also made the trip. Therefore it was no coincidence that both Pilate and Antipas were in Jerusalem when Jesus was arrested. The chief priests accused Jesus of claiming to be the Messiah. This was sufficient reason for Pilate to execute him. But for some reason he did not believe them and he did not want to get involved in a religious dispute. When he heard that Jesus was a Galilean he attempted to get the case transferred to Antipas. But Antipas did not want to get involved either and sent Jesus back to Pilate, who ordered him to be executed by the Romans.

Crime and punishment

Citizens and provincials

The governor had total power over the provincials (peregrini). This power did not extend to Roman citizens. It was forbidden to imprison, torture or execute a Roman citizen without a proper trial. As a last resort a citizen could invoke his ancient right of 'provocatio' giving him the right to trial at Rome.

Sanhedrin trials

Herod had broken the power of the Sanhedrin and taken away its right to execute. The Roman governors seem to have continued this policy. The Sanhedrin could try a Jew for a religious offence and order up to 39 lashes but they could not inflict the death penalty without the agreement of the governor. The execution of Stephen appears to have been a lynching.

Flogging

There were three types of flogging used by the Romans. The lightest form (fustes) was used as a warning to a suspected criminal. This is possibly the type Jesus received. The severer forms were usually coupled with execution.

Execution

The main forms of execution used by the Jews were stoning, strangling, beheading, burning and crucifixion. Stoning was reserved for religious offences such as blasphemy. Strangling was by garrotting. This is done with an iron collar that could be tightened. It was the punishment for a son who attacked his father. A person sentenced to be burned was buried waist deep in a pile of dung. His upper half was surrounded with tow. His mouth was forced open by two executioners who thrust a lighted torch into it. This was used for extreme sexual offences.

A roman scourge (flagrum or flagellum) reconstructed from a sculpture at Rome. It consisted of two or three thongs with pieces of bone or metal attached which ripped the skin.

ABOVE: the restored left heel complete with nail from the skeleton of a crucified man found at Giv'at ha-Mivtar.

BELOW: 1 The left shin bones showing where they were broken. 2 Lower end of the inside right ankle bone (tibia) showing where it had been cut.

1

2

B
B

ABOVE: skeleton of a foot showing where the nail went through the heel **A** and where the shin was broken **B–B**.

BELOW: 1 Right forearm bone (radius) showing where it was marked by the nail **A**.
2 Skeleton of a lower right arm showing where the nail went through.

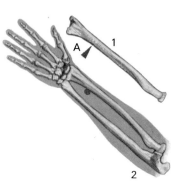

A
1

2

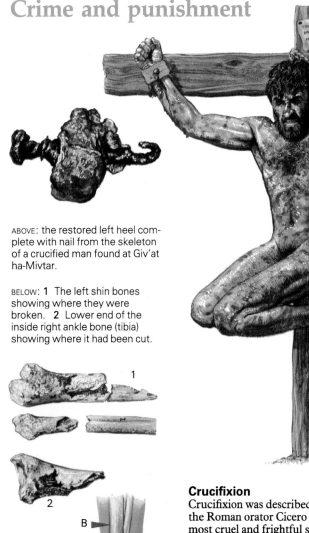

LEFT: crucifixion based on the bones from Giv'at ha-Mivtar. The nails were probably put through a plaque of wood to stop them tearing through the flesh. The weight of the body would have pulled the arm nails up the forearm to the wrist. The legs were broken against the side of the cross. All the weight of the victim's body would be on the arms causing death by suffocation.

Crucifixion

Crucifixion was described by the Roman orator Cicero as the most cruel and frightful sentence. It was inflicted for murder, banditry and piracy but most commonly for rebellion. The Romans used it on a vast scale. In Judea countless thousands went to the cross during the wars against Rome. Hadrian is said to have crucified 500 a day after the second revolt.

The ancient evidence

The victim was normally scourged and made to carry the cross-beam to the place of execution. The upright was left in position. Once the cross-beam was fixed the victim was stripped and nailed in position. Nailing was normal. There is little evidence for tying. The cross usually had a narrow strip of wood on which the victim could sit by pulling himself up. This prolonged the agony. As a special concession the Jews were allowed to remove the bodies before dark and bury them. A placard was fixed to the cross listing the victim's crimes.

The bones from Giv'at ha-Mivtar

In 1968 the bones of a crucified man were found at Giv'at ha-Mivtar just north of Jerusalem. These belonged to a man about 26 years old and 167cm (c 5' 5½") tall. The heel bones (calcanea) were still fixed together by a nail.

An examination showed that the nail had first been hammered through a piece of Pistacia or Acacia wood and then through both heel bones before entering the cross made of olive wood. The lower leg bones were broken. There was the mark of a nail on one of the lower right arm bones (radius).

The medical evidence

Medical examination showed that the arms had been nailed above the wrist and the legs broken to hasten death. The nail through the heel bones had bent and stuck fast in the wood. When the body was taken down the feet had to be cut off.

Conclusions

The angle of the breaks in the leg bones implies that the legs were bent up under the victim. From this the probable method of crucifixion can be deduced. The victim was stood up against the cross and nails hammered through his forearms. His legs were then pushed up and nailed through the heels. The weight of the body was now on his arms. The nails through the forearms tore up through the flesh until they lodged in the wrist. This sort of macabre simplicity is typically Roman. It required no skill on the part of the executioner.

The last years of Pilate

The date of the crucifixion of Jesus of Nazareth could be any time between 29 and 36 AD. The execution of their leader was a serious setback and the followers of Jesus disappear from secular history for a while.

Pilate's governorship continued to exasperate the Jews. He put pagan religious symbols on his coins which he must have known would be offensive. His failure to get the standards into Jerusalem had not discouraged him. He now tried to set up votive shields inscribed with the emperor's name. This time their reaction was not so violent. They had learned that lesson. They complained through a delegation headed by Herod's sons. When the governor refused to budge, a letter was sent to the emperor who angrily ordered Pilate to remove the offending images.

Ultimately Pilate's provocative behaviour was to cause his downfall. However, his final act was not committed against the Jews but against the Samaritans who appear to have suffered severely at his hands.

The Samaritans believed that Moses had buried the sacred Temple vessels on Mt. Gerizim. Both Jews and Samaritans lived in constant expectation of a deliverer, the Messiah. (Both John the Baptist and Jesus had been asked 'Are you the Messiah?') The Samaritans therefore responded eagerly when a would-be Messiah claimed that if the population assembled at the foot of Mt. Gerizim he would uncover the sacred vessels. As the multitudes began to assemble Pilate became uneasy. Some were armed and he feared an uprising. As the people prepared to climb the mountain he sent in his troops to disperse them and a pitched battle ensued. Many Samaritans were killed and Pilate gave orders for those taken prisoner to be executed.

The Samaritans went over Pilate's head and appealed to Vitellius the governor of Syria. Vitellius immediately marched into Judea, relieved Pilate of his office and sent him back to Rome. Having replaced Pilate temporarily with one of his own friends, Marcellus, Vitellius went up to Jerusalem. Here he was received as a hero. To make up for Pilate's excesses Vitellius remitted the taxes on fruit sold in the city and handed back custody of the sacred vestments to the high priest. Caiaphas' eighteen year term as high priest was now brought to an end. His support of Pilate had kept him his job but it had also earned him the hatred of the people. Vitellius replaced him with Jonathan a son of the ex-high priest Ananus.

ABOVE: the women of the household weaving. The woman in the foreground is rolling the coarse dyed wool as a preliminary to spinning. The girl in the background is spinning with a distaff and spindle. The older woman is weaving on an upright loom. This was the commonest form of loom at this time.

LEFT: a spindle and dyed but unspun wool from En-Gedi.
BELOW: a rug from En-Gedi.

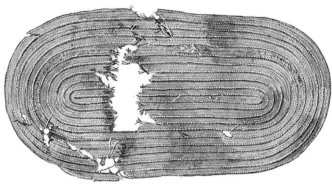

ABOVE: a rush mat from the caves at En-Gedi.

RIGHT: a detail of the same mat showing its construction. It was made in one long strip and sewn together in a spiral.

BELOW RIGHT: a bag made in the same way as the mat. This was also found at En-Gedi but similar bags were found at Masada.

BELOW: a willow basket found at En-Gedi.

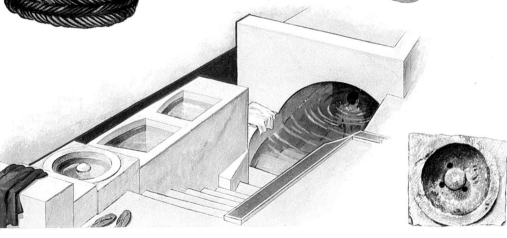

BELOW: a reconstruction of the ritual bath (mikve) from a Herodian house at Jerusalem. It was used for ritual purification in accordance with the rules of Judaism. Part of the water had to be rain water which had flowed there and not been carried. Most houses in Jerusalem had a mikve.

BELOW RIGHT: a foot bath from the same mikve

ABOVE: two boys playing the so-called 'mill game'. This was a cross between noughts and crosses and draughts.
1 A 'mill game' board. These have been found scratched on paving stones in many places including the synagogue at Capernaum.
2 Dice were very popular. This one, which was 'loaded', was found at Jerusalem.

BELOW: three lamps typical of this period from Jerusalem.

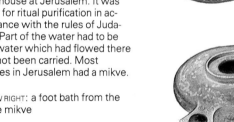

Boyhood

It was a religious duty to have children. The birth of a boy was a time of rejoicing. Eight days after birth he had to be circumcised (cutting away the foreskin of his penis). This was a sign of the agreement (covenant) made by Abraham to his god Jahweh. Circumcision was common in the middle east. The operation which was performed with a flint knife often caused pain on the third day. If he was the first born son he had to be presented in the Temple where he was offered to Jahweh as Abraham had offered his son Isaac. He was then redeemed by sacrificing two doves.

Education

At five a boy went to school. In the reign of Herod the Pharisees had begun a programme to educate every boy in the country. This was an entirely religious education. Boys were taught to read so that they could learn the scriptures. Schools were run by the local synagogue (page 71).
General education finished at 13 when a boy reached puberty and legally became a man. By then he was expected to know most if not all the scriptures by heart. Particularly bright youths could go on to further education. There were adult education classes in every village.

A girl's life

The birth of a girl was a mixed blessing. The Talmud calls them an 'illusory treasure . . . they have to be watched continually.' They had no formal education. They helped with the housework, spinning, watching the sheep etc. Children played with toys and enjoyed games. Girls even had dolls, in spite of the second commandment.

53

A maniac at Rome

Pilate sailed to Rome charged with maladministration. Before he arrived the emperor died. Tiberius' reign had not been a happy time for the Jews. In 19 AD there had been a scandal which had led to the expulsion of the Jews from Rome. Eastern religions including Judaism had become very popular amongst the women of the city. Among those attracted to the Jewish faith was a noble-woman named Fulvia. She had been persuaded by four rabbis to send a large donation to the Temple in Jerusalem. This never got further than the four rabbis. It was reported to Tiberius who had also been dealing with complaints against the Egyptian priests of Isis. As a result both Jews and Egyptians were expelled from Rome.

In 34 AD the tetrarch Philip died. As he left no male heir his realm was annexed to the province of Syria. Antipas' marriage to Herodias alienated his subjects and finally involved him in a disastrous war with his ex father-in-law the Nabataean king. Antipas suffered a crushing defeat. He turned to the emperor for help and Vitellius, governor of Syria, was sent to bale him out. Vitellius decided to strike directly at the Nabataean capital, Petra and led his army down the coast. At Acre he was met by a Jewish delegation who begged him not to lead his army through their lands because of the images on the standards they carried. Vitellius respected their wishes and sent his army south-east along the valley of Jezreel through the northern fringe of Samaria. Meanwhile he went up to Jerusalem with Antipas and they offered sacrifice in the Temple. At Jerusalem Vitellius received news of the death of Tiberius and called a halt to the campaign against the Arabs.

Caligula succeeded Tiberius in 37 AD. His reign was to prove a most difficult time for all his subjects but especially for the Jews. It had become customary to pay divine honours to emperors. In Rome this only took place after an emperor's death. However in the provinces and particularly in the east this was done during the lifetime of the emperor. It was really just a very extravagant form of homage and had very little meaning. In the east it was common to honour great men in this way, particularly after death. Alexander and the other Greek kings had all been made gods. The emperors accepted this sign of allegiance but did not try to enforce it. The difficulty arose because Caligula really believed he was a god. This, of course, presented certain problems for the Jews.

ABOVE: stone vessels found in Jerusalem. Stone-ware was popular as it was not absorbent and did not need ritual cleansing after use.

ABOVE: coloured glassware found at various sites in Israel. These did not require ritual cleansing.

1 Imported Roman tableware
2 Nabatean painted dish
3 Bronze cutlery and wooden spoon 4 Stone table and storage jar 5 Wooden plate 1–4 are from Jerusalem 5 is from En Gedi

The family

Family was the basis of Jewish society. The father was absolute head of his family. Families were much larger units than they are today. Not only did they have more children but several generations lived under the same roof. The insula at Capernaum (page 57) probably housed two families.

Relatives were expected to help each other and to do what was good for the family. Marriages were generally arranged and a bride with a large dowry would always be welcome.

It was the woman's duty to look after the home. In wealthy homes most of the work would be done by slaves but the wife was expected to spin and weave the clothes.

Divorce

Generally a man had only one wife but he could have more. A husband could divorce his wife for any reason. A divorced wife could only remarry with her ex-husband's permission. It was normal to divorce a childless wife. An unfaithful wife could be stoned to death. However there was no such punishment for unfaithful husbands.

Betrothal

Girls and boys were expected to marry as soon as they reached puberty (12½ for a girl and 14 for a boy). Marriage was preceded by a year's betrothal. During this time there would be much haggling between the families over the bride's dowry. A widow needed only to be betrothed for one month before she could remarry.

The wedding

On the eve of the wedding the bridegroom and his friends went to the bride's home to collect her. A procession was formed and the bride was carried to the bridegroom's home under a canopy made of sheets painted with gold crescents. Her long hair hung down over her shoulders and her face was veiled. The procession danced along the way and sang songs praising the bride as they carried her to her new home. That evening was spent in celebrations. A special room in the bridegroom's house had been prepared where the bride and bridesmaids could spend the night.

The following morning the celebrations continued with games, singing and dancing. That evening there was a great feast. The bride, dressed in white and bedecked with jewellery but still veiled, had the position of honour beneath the decorated canopy. The bridesmaids too were dressed in white. The bridegroom joined the bride amidst great rejoicing. Seeds were thrown at the feet of the couple or a pomegranate was crushed and a bottle of scent broken.

The bride and groom then left the celebrations to consummate their love. Only then was the bride's veil removed. Later the couple returned to the festivities which went on for seven days.

Furniture

Very little furniture has been found in the excavations in Palestine. Some stone tables were found in the recent excavations in the old Jewish quarter at Jerusalem. The rich undoubtedly had tables, chairs, beds, etc. of the type used throughout the Roman world, but most people usually sat and slept on the ground. A poor person's bed would consist of several layers of mats.

Most if not all houses had chests in which clothing and food could be kept. These could be used as tables.

On the rooftops

Most houses had flat roofs. Jews loved to eat in the open and meals were often taken up here. The roof was also used for storage.

In the warmer weather visitors slept on the roof if there was no space inside the house. There were usually steps to the roof.

ABOVE: a young wife preparing a meal. She is cutting up vegetables to boil on the stove in the background.

RIGHT: **1** Cross section of the stove shown above. This could boil two pots at once. Several of these were found at Masada. Some held as many as 8 pots. **2** Small cylindrical oven from Masada. Bread was baked in the fire. Not all these ovens had a draught hole at the bottom. **2a** Cross section of **2**.

ABOVE: **3** A stone mortarium and pestle used for crushing grain into flour. **4** A 'hopper' mortarium also used for grinding. The top part was filled with corn and rubbed backwards and forwards on a stone or wooden baseboard. **4a** Cross section of the 'hopper' **5** Iron frying pan

RIGHT: a selection of storage jars (amphorae), cooking pots and jugs discovered during the excavations at Jerusalem.

Pots, pans and plates

Cooking pots and storage jars were mainly made of clay. Crockery could be made of wood, clay, metal, stone or glass. Metal, stone and glass are not absorbent and therefore did not require ritual cleansing.

Food

Bread was the basic food. The wealthier ate wheat bread but the poorer had to make do with barley bread. Bread was broken not cut. The corn was usually ground and made into bread by the women at home. It was baked in small cylindrical ovens in which straw or dry grass and charcoal was burned.

The common people only ate meat at family feasts when a kid, calf or lamb was killed. This was usually cooked on a spit over a wood fire. The poor ate mainly fish. Pigeons were also cheap. Stews were popular – the commonest being mutton and lentil.

Cheese and butter were made from both sheep and goat's milk. Honey was used for sweetening. Salt was obtained from the Dead Sea. Locusts were considered a great delicacy. They tasted something like shrimps.

Prohibitions

Religious rules governed food as it did every other aspect of life. The pig and grazing animals that did not have cloven hooves were forbidden. The hare too was considered unclean. Animals had to be bled to death as it was forbidden to drink blood.

There were even rules on how food was to be cooked. For example lamb had to be cooked over a vine-wood fire.

Vegetables

In the country most people had kitchen gardens. Here they could grow a wide variety of vegetables such as onions, beans, leeks, peppers and melons. Most gardens had fig trees. Besides bearing two crops of fruit a year they provided shade in hot weather.

Table manners

Religion ordered that the right hand at least must be washed before meals. The food was blessed before a meal and thanks offered after it.

There were positions of honour at the 'table'. Cutlery was rare and diners dipped into large bowls of food. It was rude to dip in at the same time as someone else.

The Jews loved feasts which often went on for 5 or 6 hours. These were usually accompanied by music and dancing girls.

Houses

Agrippa

The accession of Caligula produced one unexpected consequence for the Jews. This concerned Herod's grandson Agrippa. He was the son of Alexander whom Herod had executed in 7 BC. Agrippa had spent much of his life in Rome in the hope that one day the emperor might give him a kingdom. He had squandered his wealth on parties and presents. Reduced to poverty he returned home to Judea but his creditors followed him.

Seeing no solution to his problems Agrippa decided to kill himself. His wife managed to prevent him and wrote to his sister Herodias begging for help. Herodias persuaded Antipas to give him a job as inspector of markets at Tiberias but he quarrelled with the tetrarch and had to leave. He joined the court of the governor of Syria but was found guilty of bribery and sacked.

In desperation Agrippa borrowed more money and returned to Rome. He was well received by Tiberius but news of his enormous debts followed him. To clear these he borrowed again. As each creditor demanded repayment so he was forced to borrow yet more. His debts became astronomical but his prospects had improved. He had become a close friend of Caligula. Agrippa pinned all his hopes on his new friend. He felt sure that Caligula would reward him if and when he became emperor. In his enthusiasm Agrippa let it be known that he was looking forward to the death of Tiberius. For this indiscretion he was thrown into prison where he remained for six months.

When Caligula succeeded to the throne he made Agrippa king of Philip's old realm. Agrippa was now 47 years old. He stayed on in Rome until the summer of 38 AD before setting out for his kingdom. On his way home he called in at Alexandria.

For many years there had been hostility between the Jews and Greeks in Alexandria. Caligula's insistence that he be worshipped throughout the empire gave the Alexandrian Greeks the excuse they wanted. They accused the Jews of disloyalty. Agrippa himself was mocked and taunted whilst the Jewish community were subjected to every form of degradation. The governor of the province was caught up in the surge of hatred and deprived the Jews of citizenship. Statues of the emperor were placed in the synagogues and Jews who objected were flogged or murdered. Agrippa managed to get a letter through to the emperor who gave orders for the arrest of the governor. Order was restored, but this was only the beginning.

ABOVE: The rooms at the lowest level of the 'burnt house' at Jerusalem. This was destroyed when the Romans sacked the city in 70AD. The household utensils were found in position.

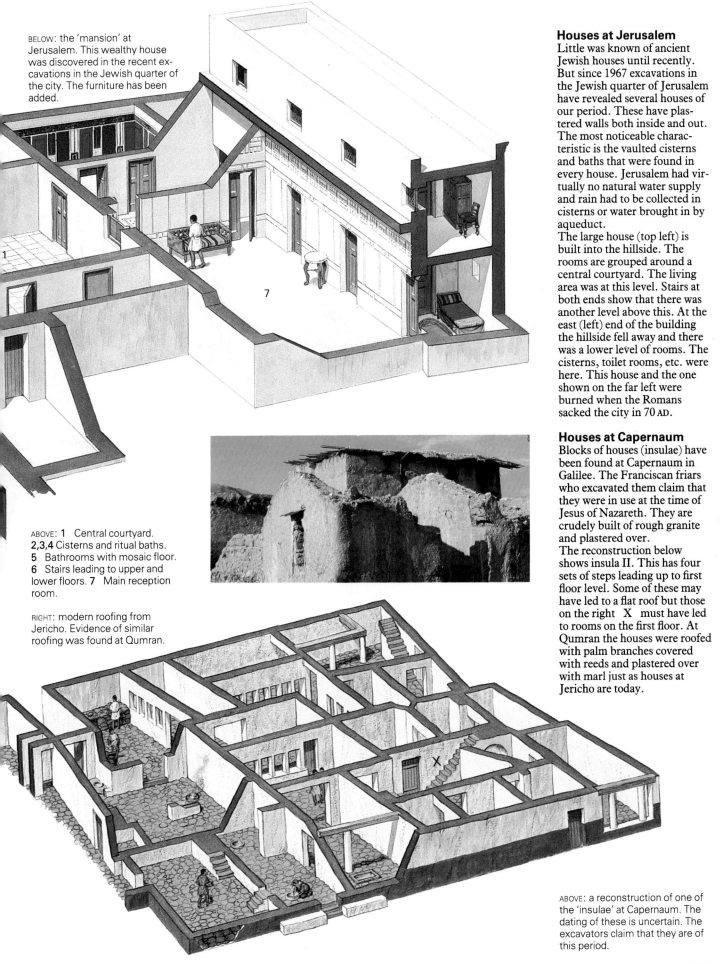

BELOW: the 'mansion' at Jerusalem. This wealthy house was discovered in the recent excavations in the Jewish quarter of the city. The furniture has been added.

ABOVE: **1** Central courtyard.
2,3,4 Cisterns and ritual baths.
5 Bathrooms with mosaic floor.
6 Stairs leading to upper and lower floors. **7** Main reception room.

RIGHT: modern roofing from Jericho. Evidence of similar roofing was found at Qumran.

Houses at Jerusalem

Little was known of ancient Jewish houses until recently. But since 1967 excavations in the Jewish quarter of Jerusalem have revealed several houses of our period. These have plastered walls both inside and out. The most noticeable characteristic is the vaulted cisterns and baths that were found in every house. Jerusalem had virtually no natural water supply and rain had to be collected in cisterns or water brought in by aqueduct.

The large house (top left) is built into the hillside. The rooms are grouped around a central courtyard. The living area was at this level. Stairs at both ends show that there was another level above this. At the east (left) end of the building the hillside fell away and there was a lower level of rooms. The cisterns, toilet rooms, etc. were here. This house and the one shown on the far left were burned when the Romans sacked the city in 70 AD.

Houses at Capernaum

Blocks of houses (insulae) have been found at Capernaum in Galilee. The Franciscan friars who excavated them claim that they were in use at the time of Jesus of Nazareth. They are crudely built of rough granite and plastered over.

The reconstruction below shows insula II. This has four sets of steps leading up to first floor level. Some of these may have led to a flat roof but those on the right X must have led to rooms on the first floor. At Qumran the houses were roofed with palm branches covered with reeds and plastered over with marl just as houses at Jericho are today.

ABOVE: a reconstruction of one of the 'insulae' at Capernaum. The dating of these is uncertain. The excavators claim that they are of this period.

Clothing

The death of a "god"

When Agrippa reached Palestine he went straight up to Jerusalem. On his release from prison on Tiberius' death Caligula had rewarded Agrippa with a gold chain of the same weight as the iron one he had worn in prison. He hung this over the treasury in the Temple as a reminder of his past troubles. His grandfather had tried to deal in an even handed way with the Jews and gentiles of his kingdom. Agrippa was of Hasmonaean descent and intended to rule as a Jew.

Caligula had given Agrippa the title of king. This cut Herodias to the core for her husband bore only the lesser title of tetrarch. She could not bear the thought of Agrippa having a higher rank than Antipas. So she began to nag him, urging him to go to Rome and demand the royal title for himself. At first Antipas wisely refused but in the end she got her way. Antipas sailed for Rome to argue his case. Instead of making him a king, the unpredictable Caligula deposed Antipas and banished him in 37 AD. It is to Herodias's credit that although she was given permission to retire to her private estate she chose to remain with her husband. As a final insult his tetrarchy was handed over to Agrippa.

In Judea the situation had become explosive. Vitellius had been replaced and the new governor of Syria, Petronius was ordered to set up the emperor's statue in the Temple at Jerusalem. With two legions Petronius advanced down the coast to Acre where he spent the winter of 39/40 AD. During the winter a vast crowd of Jews flocked to Acre to beg Petronius to reconsider. He was a reasonable man but there was little that he could do. He tried playing for time and wrote to the emperor making various excuses. In this way he managed to waste the following spring and summer. When Petronius finally ran out of excuses he wrote to the emperor begging him to withdraw the order.

In the meantime Agrippa had gone to Rome and persuaded Caligula to change his mind. Unfortunately for Petronius his letter arrived after the order had been withdrawn. Caligula had already had second thoughts. On receipt of Petronius' letter he burst into a rage and commanded him to commit suicide. The letter containing this order was held up by bad weather and took three months to get to Syria. By the time it arrived Petronius had already received news of Caligula's assassination on the 24 January 41 AD.

ABOVE: a montage of figures painted on the walls of the synagogue at Dura Europus in Syria c250AD. These show Jewish and Syrian dress in the 3rd century AD.

ABOVE: a woman's cloak reconstructed from fragments found in the caves at En Gedi. It was 2.7m long. The 'gamma' patterns in the corners can be seen on some of the women's clothes at Dura Europus. The wedge-ended stripes on the men's cloaks at Dura Europus have also been found on fragments from En Gedi.

How did Jews dress?

The second commandment forbade the painting or sculpture of the human figure. So we cannot be sure about Jewish clothing. Later these restrictions were relaxed. Some of the earliest paintings of Jews come from the synagogue at Dura Europus in Syria (c250 AD). These show Jews wearing the current fashions of the eastern Roman empire. Only a few are bearded and they are all bareheaded.

Many tunics and other pieces of clothing have been found in the caves at En Gedi. These were left by Jews involved in the 2nd revolt against Rome (c135 AD). They are very like those shown in the paintings.

Similar fragments of cloth with notched stripes and 'gamma' patterns (right, numbers 1 & 2) were found at Masada showing that similar clothes were in use by 70 AD.

The En Gedi tunics which are all different sizes confirm that Jewish men wore the knee-length tunic of the Romans and Greeks. Beards, long hair and head-dresses appear to have become optional. Only the very religious appear to have worn the old traditional costume. The majority shaved and dressed in the fashion of the day.

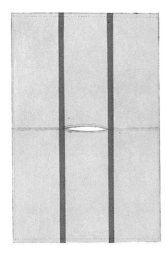

ABOVE: one of the tunics found in the caves at En Gedi. All these have two stripes. Similar fragments were found at Masada.

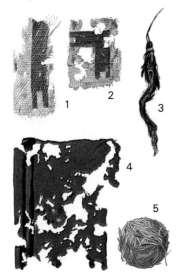

1–4 Fragments of clothing from En Gedi. 1 Notched stripe 2 Gamma pattern 3 tassel from a fringe 4 Piece of a tunic 5 Ball of wool

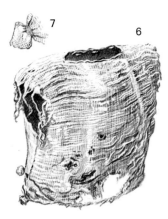

6 Boy's shirt from En Gedi 7 A little bag tied in the material. These contained such things as salt crystals and seeds to prevent illness.

8 Sandal from Masada. Almost identical sandals were discovered in the caves at En Gedi.

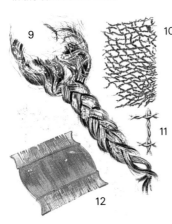

9 Plaited hair found at Masada. 10 Part of a hair net from En Gedi. 11 Detail of the hair net. 12 Bone comb from Masada.

13 Reconstructed leather drawstring purse from En Gedi. 14 How a drawstring purse was attached to the belt. 15 Reconstructed leather wallet from En Gedi.

16 Statue of a Syrian woman from Palmyra showing the love of eastern Mediterranean women for jewellery. 17 Coloured stones from En Gedi. 18 Coloured stones from Masada. 19 Earring from En Gedi. 20,21 Signet ring and fibula from Masada. 22 Jewel box with sliding bottom from En Gedi. 23 Mirror from En Gedi.

24–27 Cosmetic items. 24 Palette for mixing cosmetics. 25 Clay perfume phial. 26 Two bronze eye shadow sticks. 27 Wooden powder box. 28 Glass perfume or oil phial.

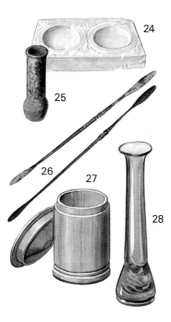

Men's clothes

The En Gedi tunics are generally made in two pieces with two stripes down the front and back. According to the Talmud the tunic was tied with a linen girdle or a hollow money belt. A rectangular cloak with a notched stripe was worn over the tunic. This may have had a fringe or tassels at the corners. The Talmud lists other garments such as underwear and a felt cap. The Greeks wore a felt cap very similar to the modern Jewish skull cap.

Women's clothes

Jewish women also appear to have worn the current fashions consisting of a long tunic tied beneath the bosom and hitched up at the waist with another girdle. It was probably sleeveless. The long sleeves of the Dura Europus paintings are 3rd century fashion. A rectangular cloak with 'gamma' patterns in the corners was worn over this. The hair was covered with a veil. Eastern women were renowned for their love of jewellery. They used cosmetics and perfumes. Many examples of these have been found.

The kingdom reunited

Agrippa was still in Rome when Caligula was assassinated and played an important part in establishing Claudius as the new emperor. As a reward Claudius gave him the whole of Herod the Great's realm. So after 45 years the area had been reunited. News of Caligula's death had been received with great joy by the Jews. Claudius sent letters to all the Jewish communities to reassure them and restore their rights. A special letter was sent to Alexandria where the Jews had suffered so greatly.

Since Herod's time the suburbs of Jerusalem had spread out to the north of the city. The people had the Roman governors to thank for this as they had improved the water supply thus making an increased population possible. Agrippa decided to enclose this 'new town' within the city walls. His building operations were reported to the governor of Syria who in turn reported it to the emperor. Ever wary of a Jewish revolt, Claudius ordered Agrippa to stop building. This wall remained half built for 25 years.

The Jews looked upon Agrippa as a mild and just ruler. He was careful to obey the letter of the Mosaic law and supported the Pharisees. He went out of his way to look after Jewish interests even outside his own territory. But his reign was to last only three years. It had become almost a custom for a new ruler to change high priests and Agrippa was no exception. In fact he changed high priests three times.

One morning at dawn Agrippa entered the theatre at Caesarea dressed in a garment woven completely of silver. The rays of the rising sun shimmerd on his clothes so that he appeared to be surrounded by an aura. His flatterers shouted out proclaiming him a god. The king did not rebuke them. Five days later he was dead. Jews and Christians were convinced that his death was a divine judgement.

When Agrippa died in 44 AD he was mourned by the Jews and reviled by the gentiles. He had fostered Pharisaic Judaism and it was inevitable that he should come into conflict with the Christian community.

Agrippa left one son, also named Agrippa who was sixteen years old. Claudius thought him too young to rule and returned the country to direct rule from Rome. For the first time Galilee came under a Roman governor, and from now on the governors bore the title of procurator and not prefect. The first procurator was Cuspius Fadus who arrived later in 44 AD.

ABOVE: an arcosolium in the tomb of Queen Helena of Adiabene at Jerusalem. This was a ledge cut into the rock wall of the tomb on which the body was laid out. The tomb was then sealed and the body left to decay.

Death
In Palestine, bodies had to be buried soon after death. The funeral was usually within 8 hours.
The body was washed and anointed with perfumes – one of the few acts permitted on the Sabbath. The dead were usually buried in their most expensive clothes. In the first century AD the rabbi Gamaliel ruled that bodies should be wrapped in white cloths. The gospels tell us that they were wrapped in shrouds containing spices, the face was covered with a cloth and the hands and feet bandaged.

The funeral procession
Male relatives carried the body on a bier with the women walking in front. There was much wailing and tearing of clothes. Often professional mourners were employed. The procession was accompanied by flute players. The Jews loved music. It was the only art they could practise freely. Painting and sculpture was forbidden.

Burial

The poor were buried simply after a family procession accompanied by two flute players. There was a communal grave for paupers in the Kedron valley outside Jerusalem. Wealthier families had tombs cut in the rock. Some of these were vast – almost like underground villages.

A simple tomb consisted normally of a rectangular room with either ledges (arcosolia) or shafts (kokim) cut in the walls. (see illustrations).

The body could either be laid out or placed in a coffin. The tomb was then sealed and the body left to decay. In the tomb shown below each of the rooms could be closed off with a stone door. The shaft graves (kokim) each had their own little door. The whole tomb complex was closed with a rolling stone as described in the gospels.

After the funeral

When the tomb was closed the door was whitewashed to warn people that there was a corrupting body there. Once the flesh had gone the bones were collected and placed in a box (ossuary).

After the funeral there would be a family meal. Mourning lasted 30 days. No work was done on the first three days. The very religious would not wash or shave and wore dirty clothes.

The rolling stone that closed the main entrance to the tomb of Queen Helena of Adiabene. The entrance to the tomb is only about a metre square. The rolling-stone type of door was either held open by a wedge and then allowed to roll down into position or it was levered into position and held there by a small stone.

ABOVE: a small anteroom (3) in the tomb of Queen Helena of Adiabene showing the entrances

to three shaft graves (kokim). The stone doors are missing but their fittings can be seen.

BELOW LEFT: a stone box (ossuary) in which the bones were placed after the flesh had decayed.

ABOVE: a stone coffin or sarcophagus found in the 'Herodian family tomb' at Jerusalem.

A section of the tomb of Queen Helena of Adiabene.
1 Main entrance closed by the rolling stone.
2 Large antechamber with doors leading off to the various tomb chambers.

3 Smaller antechamber giving access to the shaft graves (kokim) number 4 and the arcosolia chamber number 5. This picture shows only one small part of the tomb complex. Each section has its own small antechamber with the tomb chambers and shaft graves around it.

Craftsmen

The rise of the Zealots

The rule of Cuspius Fadus and that of his successor Tiberius Alexander, a non-religious Jew from Alexandria, were fairly uneventful. On the orders of the emperor, Fadus tried to repossess the high priest's vestments in order to give the Romans a stranglehold on the priesthood. The Jews protested and were allowed to send a deputation to Rome. The young Agrippa put their case to Claudius and the emperor withdrew the order.

The return of the Romans led to a revival of the popularity of the Zealots. The inclusion of the unruly Galileans within the Roman province must have increased the tension, which was aggravated by a famine. The Messiah problem was a constant nightmare to the Romans. When yet another one appeared the procurator followed the normal procedure and sent in the cavalry. The 'deliverer' was captured and crucified. As far as the Romans were concerned another uprising had been avoided.

Josephus mentions only this one uprising but records that Tiberius Alexander crucified James and Simon the sons of Judas the Galilean who had founded the Zealot movement.

The situation was made infinitely worse by an incident in 48 AD when Cumanus was procurator. It was caused by a stupid but typical act of a Roman auxiliary soldier. It was Passover. The Temple platform was crowded with pilgrims. As usual the Roman garrison in the Antonia fortress had descended on to the porticoes to discourage trouble. One of the soldiers, no doubt expressing the opinion of his comrades, pulled up his tunic and presented his bare backside to the crowd and made the appropriate vulgar noise. The effect was devastating. The crowds turned on the soldiers and began to stone them. Cumanus over-reacted and sent in reinforcements. In the stampede some stumbled and others tripped over them and literally thousands were trampled to death.

This led to protests and several minor incidents. A soldier lost his temper, tore up and burned a sacred scroll. Cumanus defused this situation by executing the soldier, but his problems were far from over.

Some Galileans were killed on their way through Samaria. The incident was reported to Cumanus but he ignored it. When the news reached Jerusalem the mob burst into a frenzy of hatred against the Samaritans. Led by two Zealots they invaded Samaria.

ABOVE: **1** Roman sculpture showing a bow-saw and blade. **2** An iron saw blade.

BELOW: A reconstruction of a carpenter's workshop. This is set in a block of houses (insulae) similar to the type excavated at Capernaum.

Workers and slaves
The Jews considered work noble and it was no disgrace to do menial jobs. The poverty of Palestine was proverbial. Consequently there were few slaves. Nearly all back-breaking and unpleasant jobs were done by free men. Slaves generally were owned only by the rich. The servants in the New Testament were slaves. Obviously some jobs were considered nobler than others. Sandal-making and woodworking were considered good trades – smelly jobs such as tanning were not. Tanneries had to be outside a town and down wind of it. Perfume sellers were considered disreputable.

Roman iron tools: **1** Chisel
2 Gouge **3** Draw knife **4** Hand saw **5** Axe-head **6** Hammer-head **7** Plane (This is remarkably similar to the modern tool.)

Craftsmen

Jewish craftsmen were much the same as those in other parts of the ancient world. The prohibition on human or animal representation stilted the growth of painting, carving and sculpture. When a high standard was required craftsmen usually had to be brought in from outside Palestine or the goods themselves imported. Native carpenters and masons did the more basic work.

A Jewish boy was automatically apprenticed to his father and learned his trade as he grew up. The various tradesmen wore symbols of their trade. For example, a carpenter wore a chip of wood behind his ear, a tailor had a needle stuck in his tunic and a dyer wore a coloured rag. These symbols were forbidden on the sabbath.

The tools shown on this page all come from the western half of the Roman Empire but similar instruments must have been used in the eastern half.

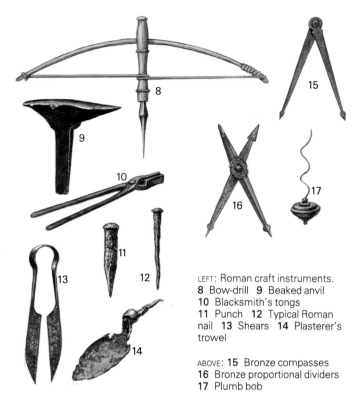

LEFT: Roman craft instruments.
8 Bow-drill **9** Beaked anvil
10 Blacksmith's tongs
11 Punch **12** Typical Roman nail **13** Shears **14** Plasterer's trowel

ABOVE: **15** Bronze compasses
16 Bronze proportional dividers
17 Plumb bob

Another bad governor

Cumanus raced from Caesarea with his Sebastene cavalry and fell upon the invading mob. Many were killed or captured. In the meantime the Samaritans had sent a deputation to Quadratus the governor of Syria. The Jews also appealed to him claiming that Cumanus had been bribed by the Samaritans. Quadratus carried out a careful investigation which convinced him that an uprising was being planned by the Jews. He ordered the crucifixion of all the Jewish prisoners and beheaded five others who had been involved in the massacre. The Jewish and Samaritan leaders together with Cumanus were sent to Rome to put their case to the emperor. Agrippa once again interceded for them. Claudius probably considered that the Jews had paid sufficiently for their crime and released them. Three of the leading Samaritans were executed and Cumanus banished. About 50 AD Agrippa, who was now about 22, was given his kingdom. In 53 AD Claudius transferred him to the much larger realm of his uncle Philip to the north-east of the Sea of Galilee.

Claudius replaced Cumanus with Antonius Felix. The choice seems strange. Felix was one of the emperor's ex-slaves. This did not necessarily mean that he lacked the education and skill to administer a province. Many slaves were far better educated than their masters. The incredible thing is that Felix should have been given Judea. Felix was the first freedman to hold such a job. His administration was to prove an unmitigated disaster.

In 54 AD Claudius died. He was succeeded by the infamous Nero. The new emperor confirmed Felix in his post and increased the realm of the young Agrippa giving him control over certain towns in Peraea and Galilee including Antipas' old capital Tiberias.

Felix's misgovernment played straight into the hands of the Zealots. Daily the movement gained more and more influence with the common people. Felix became very disturbed at their increased popularity and arranged a meeting with their leader Eleazar. In spite of a promise of safe conduct Felix shipped Eleazar and his companions off to Rome to stand trial. Having got rid of their leader he launched a campaign against the Zealots and their sympathisers. Hundreds, perhaps thousands, were crucified or imprisoned. Many innocent people suffered the same fate which only served to increase anti-Roman feeling and the influence of the Zealots.

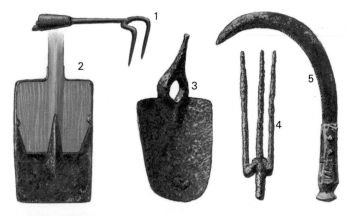

ABOVE: **1–3** Roman agricultural instruments **4** An Iron winnowing fork from Lachish **5** An iron sickle with wooden handle from En Gedi

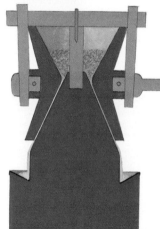

BELOW: a corn mill. This type of mill was used all over the Roman world. Examples can be seen at Capernaum and Qumran.
LEFT: cross-section of a corn mill. The grain was tipped in at the top. The top half of the mill was turned and the grain ground into flour against the cone-shaped lower part.

Ploughing and sowing

Fields were ploughed after the autumn rains had softened the ground. They were ploughed at least once along and once across leaving an even surface. The corn was scattered (broadcast) and ploughed or harrowed in.

Harvesting

The corn was reaped with sickles. It was then taken to an area of hardened ground (threshing floor) where the grain was beaten (flailed) or trodden out by cattle. Alternatively a heavy wooden board with flint teeth on the underside (threshing sledge) could be used. The corn was then winnowed – thrown up in the air to allow the wind to blow away the chaff.

Grapes and olives

Grapes were normally trodden in a vat about 2m square to squeeze out the juice. Oil was crushed out of the olives either by stone rollers as shown below or with a press. Presses were operated either by a screw or a lever.

The calendar

The Jewish calendar was based on lunar months. It had only 354 days to a year and had to be corrected continually. 'The corn is not ripe so we have added an extra month this year.'
Farmers required a more accurate system and used the stars to estimate the seasons. They had to know when to sow vegetables.

RIGHT: 1 Stone olive mill reconstructed from parts found at Capernaum. This was used to squeeze the oil out of the olives.

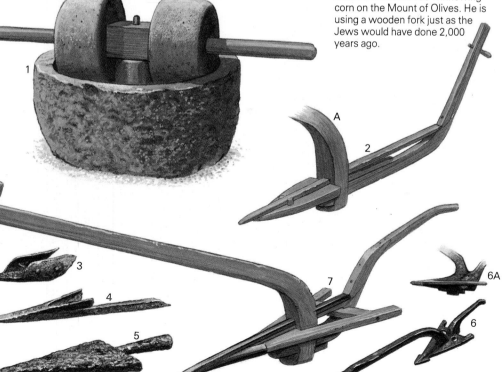

ABOVE: a modern Arab winnowing corn on the Mount of Olives. He is using a wooden fork just as the Jews would have done 2,000 years ago.

RIGHT: 2 an ancient wooden plough found in Denmark. The beam **A** is made of birch wood. The other parts are oak. All the parts are socketed into the beam.
3–5 Roman iron plough shares
6 Model of a Roman plough
6a Side view of the model
7 Reconstruction of a Roman plough for use with two oxen

Assassins and Messiahs

Felix's campaign drove the Zealots underground, but the struggle was continued by the Sicarii. The Sicarii were even more fanatical than the Zealots. They were an assassination squad. They were called Sicarii because of the short curved daggers (sicae) which they carried under their garments. During festivals they mingled with the crowd and stabbed those who were suspected of Roman sympathies. Their most notable victim was Jonathan the high priest.

Naturally the rising tension produced a crop of Messiahs. Felix dealt with them in the usual Roman way by sending in the cavalry. The most famous of these Messiahs was an Egyptian Jew who led his followers on to the Mount of Olives claiming that God would throw down the walls of Jerusalem and hand over the city to him. His words were cut short when Felix led his heavy infantry against the mob, backed up by the population of Jerusalem. Most of the Egyptian's followers were killed but he escaped.

Shortly after this Paul seems to have been involved in a riot on the Temple platform and was arrested by the Roman garrison from the Antonia. The centurion in command thought Paul was the Egyptian. The story in the Acts of the Apostles tells how Paul was on the point of being flogged when he declared that he was a Roman citizen. He was then dispatched to Caesarea to stand trial before the governor.

The failure of the Messiahs drove their followers to support the Zealots. The chief priests had become mere puppets of the Romans. They were utterly corrupt and began seizing the tithes due to the ordinary priests. As a result some of the poorer priests were dying of starvation. This drove many of them into the Zealot camp.

The new nationalistic spirit even spread to Caesarea. Fights broke out between the Jewish and Syrian elements in the city. The Jews were in a minority but claimed superiority because Herod had founded the city. This probably meant that the Jews wanted to impose Jewish law on the gentile population. Felix broke up the riots and sent a deputation from both sides to Rome leaving the emperor to sort things out.

Felix had angered the Jews by his marriage to Drusilla the sister of Agrippa. She had been married to the king of Emesa but Felix had persuaded her to desert the king and marry him. It was not the desertion that angered the Jews but the fact that Felix was uncircumcised.

ABOVE LEFT: the Jordan valley about 20km south of the Sea of Galilee. The hills of the Decapolis can be seen in the background.

BELOW LEFT: the river Jordan at the same spot as above.

ABOVE: Tiberias, the city built by Herod's son Antipas on the west shore of the Sea of Galilee. The ruins of the ancient city can still be seen in the modern city.

RIGHT: Fishermen casting their nets at dawn on the Sea of Galilee as they have done for thousands of years.

RIGHT BOTTOM: the southern end of the Dead Sea.

Near anarchy

About 60 AD Felix was replaced by Festus. Soon after Festus' arrival in Palestine the deputations of Jews and Syrians from Caesarea returned from Rome. Nero had given judgement in favour of the Syrian majority. The Jews had hoped to take over the city but now they lost even their equality.

Not a great deal is known about the rule of Festus. The economic crisis which had begun some 30 years earlier appears to have gradually worsened. This aggravated the political situation. The assassinations of the Sicarii continued and there was yet another Messiah making the usual claims. He and his flock were massacred by the Roman forces. In the Acts of the Apostles we are told that shortly after Festus had assumed office Paul was brought before him. He had been held prisoner in Caesarea for two years. He now exercised his right as a Roman citizen and was accordingly sent to Rome to stand trial.

Festus' rule lasted only two years as he died in office. There was a gap of some months between the death of Festus and the arrival of the new governor and the current high priest Ananus seized the opportunity to destroy his enemies. Amongst these was the Christian community at Jerusalem. On his order James the brother of Jesus, together with other non-conformists, was dragged out and stoned to death. Complaints were made to Agrippa who promptly deposed Ananus.

The actions of Ananus were symptomatic of the time. Law and order was breaking down. The situation was not helped by the arrival of a new governor, Albinus. He was weak and an appeaser. All sides soon realised that he could be bribed. The Zealots and Sicarii flourished under him.

When the poorer priests objected to their tithes being stolen they were flogged. Agrippa tried to solve matters by changing the high priest again. He nominated Jesus the son of Damneus but soon had second thoughts and replaced him with another Jesus, the son of Gamaliel. The first Jesus refused to accept his dismissal and the two of them, backed up by hired thugs, fought pitched battles in the streets of Jerusalem. In the end Agrippa disowned them both and gave the office to Matthias.

The final catastrophe was approaching fast but nobody seemed to notice – nobody that is except yet another Jesus, the son of Ananias. He arrived in Jerusalem in the autumn of 62 AD and began prophesying doom to the city.

Jew or Christian
Christianity spread rapidly both inside and outside Palestine. Wherever there were Jewish communities the new sect gained ground. At first it was just a sect of Judaism to which only Jews could belong. But soon, like Judaism, it was attracting gentile converts.

LEFT: a portrait of Nero

BELOW: the eastern Roman Empire showing Paul's journeys. Christianity must also have spread to the Jewish communities of Babylon and the north African coast.

Conversion of the gentiles

The possibility of converting the gentiles inspired many of the Jews of the Diaspora and Paul of Tarsus embarked on a mission to the gentiles c 47–61 AD. This change of direction was condemned by the Christian leaders at Jerusalem who insisted that converts must be circumcised and obey the Law. This produced dissension within the Church.

The mission to the gentiles proved so successful that by the mid-sixties Christians could be distinguished from Jews and were persecuted. The influence of the Jerusalem church disappeared when the city was sacked by the Romans in 70 AD and Christianity became an independent religion.

RIGHT: the site of the harbour at Caesarea. It was from here that Paul was taken to Rome.

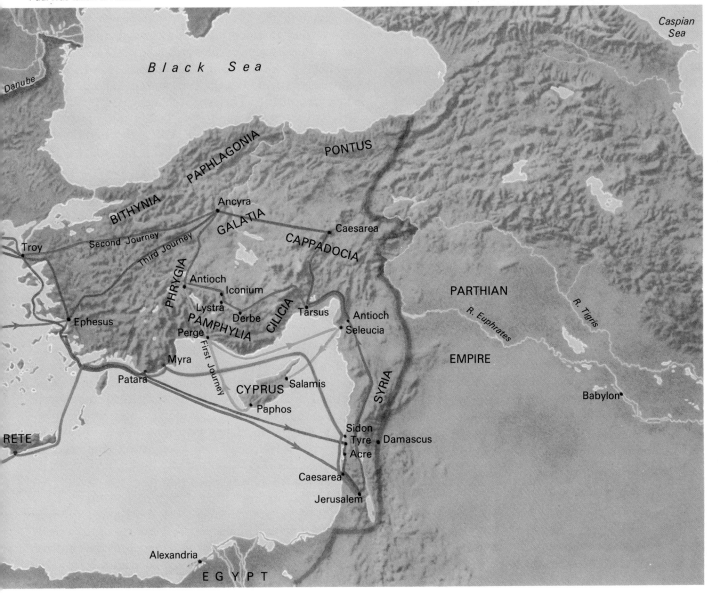

The rising storm

The position of the Jewish community in Rome had improved since the time of Tiberius. Many noble women had come under Jewish influence, including Poppaea Nero's wife. A considerable Christian community had also grown up there. The ordinary Roman looked upon both groups with suspicion and distaste.

In 64 AD part of Rome was destroyed by fire. Thousands were made homeless. In their anger the people pointed accusing fingers at Nero. His building plans were well known and the fire conveniently cleared the way for them. Nero looked round for a scapegoat. Both Jews and Christians were distrusted and it would not be difficult to divert public anger in their direction. Poppaea's attachment to the Jews saved them. It was the Christians who paid. Many were flung to the wild beasts in the Circus Maximus. Others were burned as torches in the imperial gardens.

In Judea the dire predictions of Jesus son of Ananias continued. Day and night he cried out his warnings in the streets. When he refused to be silent he was hauled before the Sanhedrin and flogged. But still he persisted. He was brought before the governor who asked him who he was and where he came from. Jesus gave no answer. The governor had him scourged to the bone and released declaring him insane. But still his voice echoed through the city – 'Woe to Jersusalem!'

Under Albinus law and order eventually collapsed. Nero tried to correct matters by sending out a strict authoritarian, Gessius Florus, a 'hanger and flogger' who believed in putting down the slightest disturbance with the utmost severity. But violence only bred violence. When Cestius Gallus, the governor of Syria, came to Jerusalem for the Passover the Jews begged him to relieve their misery. But Gallus did nothing.

The enmity between the Jews and Syrians at Caesarea flared up again. This time it was over a piece of land adjoining the synagogue on which the Syrians wanted to erect workshops. When the Jews caused a disturbance Florus threw their leaders in to prison.

There was an outcry at Jerusalem but no rioting. Hardly had feelings cooled than Florus sent to Jerusalem to withdraw money from the Temple treasury, claiming it was needed for public works. No one believed him. There was much grumbling and some young wags carried round baskets collecting 'pennies for poor Florus'. In anger the governor advanced on the city with his forces.

On arriving at Jerusalem Florus set up his tribunal in front of the palace and demanded the surrender of those who had insulted him. When the Jews refused Florus turned his soldiers loose. Many of the citizens caught up in the stampede for safety were trampled or killed by the soldiers. Others were captured, scourged and crucified.

The following a day a demonstration was held outside the city, opposite the palace. Two cohorts of Roman troops were coming up the road from Caesarea. They had been warned to be ready for trouble. They drew their clubs and began beating back the demonstrators. The crowds were enormous and the troops must have realised that if they were attacked in the open they would be overwhelmed. They tried to force their way through the gate and across the city to the Antonia. In the narrow streets the soldiers were jostled by the angry crowd. Florus unwisely ordered out the troops in the palace to try to clear the street. This was the final straw. Violence erupted. Stones began to fly. Youths now climbed up on to the roofs and began pelting the soldiers with stones. The soldiers could make no headway and retreated to the palace.

The crowds now turned on the Antonia. They were frightened that the garrison might try to occupy the Temple platform. Finding the soldiers still in the fortress they broke down the adjoining porticoes thus cutting off the garrison from the Temple area.

Florus was getting worried. He knew that if there was a full-scale uprising he would be cut off in Jerusalem. He called in the chief priests and offered to withdraw to Caesarea leaving only a single cohort in the city. They agreed provided that it was not the same cohort that had attacked the people.

Both sides wrote to Cestius Gallus the governor of Syria who sent a tribune to investigate. On his way to Jerusalem the tribune met up with Agrippa who was returning from abroad and told him what was happening in Jerusalem. They went up to the city together. The crowd welcomed the young king. But when it became clear that he only wanted to try and reconcile the two sides they expelled him from the city.

The Zealots knew that their time had come. They seized Masada and slaughtered the Roman garrison there. In Jerusalem they gained control of the priests and the daily sacrifice that was offered for the emperor ceased. It was the final act of defiance.

The Synagogue

The feasts of the Lord
There were five main religious holy days – Passover, Feast of Weeks (Pentecost), Harvest Festival (Tabernacles), Feast of Trumpets on the 7th new moon of the year and the Day of Atonement. There were other feasts and, of course, the Sabbath days.

The Sabbath
When the first three stars appeared on Friday evening the Sabbath trumpet was sounded calling people from their work. The Sabbath had begun. Supper was now served. The Law forbade the normal household chores on the Sabbath. All meals had to be prepared on Friday. No more food was eaten until after the Synagogue service the following morning.

At the Synagogue
The Synagogue had no priests and no sacrifices. It was run by an elected committee.
The service began with prayers recited by one man standing before the Torah Ark – a cupboard containing the sacred scrolls of the Law. The congregants joined in the recitation of the prayers. When praying, a Jewish male wrapped himself in a prayer shawl. For the morning weekday service he would put on phylacteries, fastened in the prescribed manner around the forehead and left arm, which contained scriptural passages that were reminders of the obligation to keep the Law.

The sermon
After the prayers one of the scrolls was taken from the Ark and given to the first of seven readers. The texts were read in a strict rota so that the whole Law could be read within a set period. The text was in Hebrew. This was not the spoken language of the people. The Jews spoke Aramaic which had been the universal language of the old Persian empire. When the reader had finished he sat down and gave a sermon on the text in Aramaic. Anyone could perform this duty. No qualifications were required. Alms were collected at the door as the congregation left. At twilight the trumpet sounded again. The Sabbath was over.

Masada and Herodium
No certain example of a synagogue of this period exists but at both Masada and Herodium buildings have been discovered which may have been synagogues. However, neither of these buildings faces Jerusalem, the traditional orientation of synagogues.

BELOW: **1** The original plan of the synagogue at Masada. **2** The Masada synagogue showing the changes made by the Zealots with benches along the walls. **3** Plan of the synagogue at Herodium. **M** = Mikve **N** = North **J** = The direction of Jerusalem

ABOVE: Herod's dining room at Herodium which was converted into a synagogue by the Zealots. They put in columns, benches of masonry along the walls and a mikve at the front. The reconstruction shows the Torah Ark opposite the door with the reader's platform in front. The congregation are seated listening to the sermon.

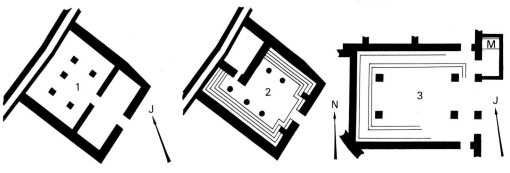

3

WOE TO THEE JERUSALEM

The defeat of Cestius Gallus

News of the revolt spread like wildfire. Zealots and Sicarii poured into the city, swelling the ranks of the rebels. They attacked the upper city where the pro-Romans had taken refuge. The defenders were unable to withstand the assault and were forced to withdraw to the palace citadel.

The rebels now turned on the Antonia, the very symbol of Roman oppression. They stormed the fortress and massacred the garrison. The auxiliary Roman troops holding the upper palace realised that their position was hopeless. They retreated to the three massive towers that Herod had built at the north end of the citadel leaving the pro-Roman faction to their fate. The next day the palace fell. The high priest was captured and killed by the rebels. The garrison in the citadel towers held out as long as they could. In the end they surrendered on the guarentee of safe conduct out of the area, but were cut down by the rebels.

The revolt at Jerusalem released all the old pent up hatred. All over the country Jews and gentiles slaughtered each other. Towns were sacked and burned. Populations were wiped out. In Alexandria the legions had to be brought in to protect the Greeks. This of course resulted in a massacre of the Jews.

Cestius Gallus the governor of Syria moved down to Acre with about a third of his forces. He occupied Caesarea and Joppa so that he could be supplied from the sea. Then he marched into Galilee which was subdued with comparative ease. He then advanced on Jerusalem capturing and burning the unwalled northern suburbs of the city.

But winter was fast approaching and the countryside was still in enemy hands. Gallus knew that he could not embark on a lengthy siege. His supply lines would be constantly threatened. He made an attempt to capture the Temple but when this failed he decided to withdraw.

The Jews immediately went on to the offensive. Swarming through the hills they attacked the retreating column at every opportunity. Whilst on open ground the Romans were able to beat off the attacks. When they began the descent along the hills towards Beth Horon the Jews launched an all-out attack on the baggage train driving it down into the valley. The main part of the Roman army managed to escape during the night but they were forced to abandon the baggage train with all their siege equipment.

The Jews pursued the retreating column all the way to the coastal plain where the Romans could have brought their cavalry into play. The Jews called off the pursuit and returned to Jerusalem in triumph dragging the siege weapons with them.

The defeat of Cestius Gallus. Having driven the Roman baggage train down into the valley near Beth Horon the Jews close in for the kill. The Roman cavalry try to drive them off but they are overwhelmed by the ferocity of the Jewish attack.

Vespasian takes over

But the Jews totally underestimated the power of Rome. At Jerusalem the old walls were repaired. The north wall which Agrippa had started was completed. Locked up in their walled cities they thought they could withstand any Roman assault. It was to be a war without battles against an enemy who were the absolute masters of siege warfare.

The extreme nationalists, the Zealots and the Sicarii did not have a great following and the generals selected were all moderates. Among these was a young priest named Joseph. This was the Josephus who later wrote a history of the Jewish War. The moderates were never fully committed to the revolt. They lived in the hope that they could find a peaceful settlement.

Josephus was given command of Galilee and the Golan heights. From the beginning his authority was challenged by a Zealot leader, John of Gishchala. And the Galileans distrusted Josephus. He tried to organise a disciplined army but because of his lack of conviction he failed to inspire his troops.

Meanwhile Gallus had sent a report to Nero who was in Greece. In the spring of 67 AD Vespasian was given command of the war. He was now in his late fifties and a very experienced commander. He had been decorated for his service as commander of the Second Legion, called Augusta, during the conquest of Britain twenty years earlier. Vespasian sent his 27 year old son Titus to Alexandria to mobilize the Fifteenth Legion whilst he went to Syria to pick up the Fifth and Tenth Legions. He then moved down the coast to Acre.

Josephus had failed to unite the Galileans. Sepphoris the largest city in the area went over to the Roman side the moment Vespasian arrived. The town was given a garrison of 6,000 infantry and 1,000 cavalry. These caused havoc amongst Josephus' forces. When Titus arrived with the Fifteenth Legion Vespasian was ready to start the campaign. Including his auxiliary forces he had over 50,000 men.

When Vespasian advanced on Galilee Josephus' field army deserted him and Josephus himself fled to Tiberias. The Romans began the reconquest in their usual thorough way. The city of Gabara in Upper Galilee was stormed, the adult male population was killed and the town reduced to ashes. All the towns and villages in the area were burned and any people captured were sold into slavery.

ABOVE: bronze scales from Masada (actual size). About 400 of these scales with the remains of tinning on them were found. They probably belonged to the Zealots.

BELOW: **1** Sword found in a house at Jerusalem **2** Arrow head from Masada (actual size) **2a** Section of **2** **3** Part of an arrow from Masada **4** Part of an arrow from En Gedi **1** scale 1:10 **3** and **4** scale 1:4

The Zealots
The Zealots were a splinter group of the Pharisees. The Pharisees were content to ignore the Romans. The Zealots were not. They wanted to drive them out. They planned to establish the Kingdom of Heaven on earth – a kingdom ruled by God and not by man. When Jesus said 'Render unto Caesar the things that are Caesar's and to God the things that are God's', the Zealots would have agreed with him. For all the produce of God's land belonged to God and this included the Roman tribute. The main Zealot centre was Galilee. The revolt really started when Galilee was annexed to the Roman province in 44 AD.

The leaders of the revolt
When the war began the Jews turned not to the Zealots but to their traditional leaders. These were the very people who had collaborated with the Romans. Most of them had no heart for the war and tried to make peace. They were opposed by the Zealots who wanted war. The future historian, Josephus, was sent to command Galilee. His performance was pathetic. The hardy Galileans should have been the backbone of the revolt. But he could neither inspire nor unite them. In Jerusalem it was only after many assassinations and massacres that natural leaders emerged. By then it was too late.

Armour and weapons
The Zealots must have had hidden stores of weapons but most Jews possessed none at all. Several hundred Roman soldiers were massacred at the outbreak of the war and many more died during the retreat of Cestius Gallus. The victory yielded a small supply of armour and weapons. More were found in the royal armoury at Masada. The simple bow seems to have been the main weapon. Many arrow heads were found amongst the debris at Masada.

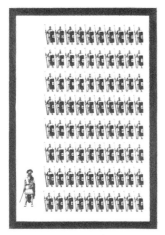

Century

Hastatus prior	Hastatus posterior
Princeps prior	Princeps posterior
Pilus prior	Pilus posterior

6 centuries = 1 cohort

ABOVE: a legionary century commanded by a centurion. A cohort was made up of six centuries.

BELOW: **1** Typical Roman mail made of iron rings (actual size). Alternate rows are riveted.
2 Roman bronze scale armour (actual size). The scales were wired to each other and then sewn on to a cloth backing.

BELOW: a typical Roman sword and scabbard of the later first century AD. The blade was about 50cm long. This was primarily used for thrusting and not cutting.

ABOVE: a reconstruction of an eastern legionary of the second half of the first century AD. He wears a tinned bronze helmet and mail shirt. He is armed with a heavy javelin, sword and dagger. His shield is made of wood covered with hide and has a metal boss.

BELOW: **3** The type of armour worn by the legionaries in the west. It is uncertain whether this type (lorica segmentata) was used in the east. **4** A bronze helmet found in the river Po near Cremona in Italy. This may have been lost by one of the eastern legionaries when Vitellius was defeated.

The Roman forces

The Romans had nine legions concentrated in the east. There were also 60–70 auxiliary units in the area. The armies of the client kings were obliged to serve with the Roman army if required. In all some 100,000 troops were available. Vespasian called out about half these. He advanced southwards from Syria with two legions – the Fifth, (called Macedonica) and the Tenth (Fretensis) whilst his son Titus brought up the Fifteenth (Deiotariana) from Egypt. They were accompanied by about 17,000 auxiliary infantry and 5,500 cavalry. The local client kings (including Agrippa II) supplied 4,000 cavalry and some 10,000 archers. The total Roman forces amounted to about 32,000 infantry, 10,000 archers and 10,000 cavalry.

The legions

Legions were composed of foot soldiers holding Roman citizenship. They were professionals who had signed on for 25 years. A legion consisted of ten cohorts divided into six centuries of about 80 men. Each century was commanded by a centurion. About 120 cavalry were attached to each legion, making a total of about 5,000.

Armour and weapons

Legionaries were armed with heavy javelins (pila) and short thrusting swords. Each legionary also carried a small dagger. A legionary's armour consisted of a helmet and mail shirt made up of small iron rings. Some wore armour of overlapping metal scales. A new type of armour made of iron plates was in use in the west. It is uncertain whether it had been adopted in the east. The legionary also carried a large curved wooden shield.

The auxiliaries

The auxiliary forces were drawn from the provincials who did not have citizenship. These could be any type of soldier – light infantry, cavalry, archers, or slingers. Foot soldiers were organised into cohorts like the legionaries. These could either be 500 or 1,000 strong. Cavalry were organised in alae of similar sizes. Most of the auxiliary infantry and cavalry used a flat oval shield about a metre long. Cavalrymen used a long slashing sword and a spear or javelin.

The siege of Jotapata

The ravaging of the countryside certainly had the desired effect on Josephus who wrote a letter to Jerusalem asking if he should surrender. He then moved to Jotapata about 7km west of Gabara possibly hoping to disrupt the Roman supply lines. When Vespasian was informed he sent 1,000 cavalry to blockade the town and followed up with the rest of the army. Jotapata was built on a cliffy spur jutting out from a hill. It could only be approached from the top of a hill. This made it very difficult to assault.

Vespasian moved up all his artillery, backed by his archers, javelineers and slingers. These kept up a constant barrage against the defenders whilst the legionaries constructed a ramp which would bring them up to the level of the battlements. The Jews countered this in the usual way by increasing the height of the walls.

The sight of the Roman ramp was too much for Josephus and he decided to get out while he still could. He laid his plans in secret but the townspeople found out what he was up to. He tried to convince them that he was too important to risk capture. He talked desperately of relieving forces and diversions but they insisted that he stayed.

When the ramp reached a sufficient height the Romans moved up a battering ram and began to pound the wall. The defenders tried to cushion the blows by hanging sacks of chaff in front of the ram but the Romans used sickles on long poles to cut the ropes by which the sacks were suspended. Finally the defenders managed to break off the head of the ram with a boulder. They then set light to its housing. The Romans were unable to put out the fire but managed to save the ram itself. The town had gained a short respite, but by evening the ram was at work again. The pounding continued right through the night. Shortly before dawn a part of the wall collapsed. Soon after daylight, amidst blaring trumpets and thunderous war cries, the legionaries attacked, but they were driven back.

Vespasian called off the attack and began to erect three iron clad towers from which a constant barrage could be directed against the defenders on the wall. The ramp was heightened until it overtopped the battlements. Just before dawn on the 47th day of the siege the Romans broke into the town. They killed every living thing. Josephus claims that 40,000 died in the siege. The town itself was flattened.

Josephus and 40 of the leading citizens were hiding in a cave. When they were discovered Josephus tried to surrender but his comrades stopped him. He explained to them that it was God's will that he should survive but they were unimpressed. It was decided that they should commit mass suicide. Josephus agreed. It comes as no surprise that he was the last man left alive. He surrendered to the Romans and in return for betraying his people he was spared.

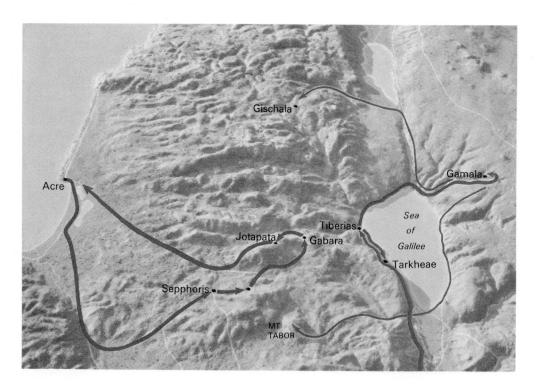

LEFT: model map showing Vespasian's campaigns in Galilee (67 AD). The main troop movements are shown by broad red arrows and lesser movements by thin red arrows.
Sepphoris had surrendered and Vespasian used it to give him a safe route into the Galilean hills. Josephus and his forces were at Garis but they fled before the Romans even came in sight. Vespasian stormed Gabara and then turned on Jotapata where Josephus had taken refuge. The town fell after a siege of 47 days and Vespasian returned to Acre. The second campaign was launched up the Jordan valley. Tiberias surrendered and the remainder of the Jewish forces were defeated at Taricheae. The Romans now laid siege to Gamala. Troops were sent from here to capture Mount Tabor and Gischala.

Roman siege techniques 1: ramps

RIGHT: The site of Jotapata. The town was built on the low hill in the middle distance (in the centre of the picture). It could only be approached from the hill behind it.

Roman siege tactics

The Romans used two methods for besieging towns. The first was the blockade. A wall was built round the town to keep all the defenders in and all help out. The town was then starved into surrender.

If a quick result was needed a ramp was constructed so that siege engines such as battering rams and mobile towers could be moved up to the wall. The wall would then be battered down and the town stormed.

Building a ramp

The ramp was made of earth and rubble held together at the sides by logs. The logs were fastened together as shown on the far right and filled with rubble. These 'walls' were constructed at the same time as the ramp and prevented the 'fill' spreading outwards.

The men working on the ramp were protected by sheds and wicker screens. These were covered with hides as a protection against fire. Open-ended sheds 5 metres long and 2.5 metres high were placed end to end to form long tunnels through which materials could be brought up in safety.

LEFT: the legionary's tools.
1 basket 2 pickaxe 3 mattock. The Roman general Corbulo claimed that more wars were won with the pickaxe than the sword.

4 A section of a ramp showing its timber 'walls'. It was filled with rubble and earth. 5 The structure of the timber 'walls'. When filled with rubble these were exceedingly strong.

BELOW: The assault on Jotapata. The ramp probably ended at the ditch in front of the wall. This was then filled with rubble so that the ram could be moved up.

1 Original wall 2 New wall built during the siege 3 Battering ram 4 Covered passageways 5 Archers 6 Light sharp-shooting catapults 7 Heavy stone-throwing catapults

The fall of Galilee

Vespasian now gave his troops a few weeks rest whilst he and Titus went to see Agrippa at Caesarea Philippi. Here Titus met Agrippa's sister Berenice. She was Herod's great grand-daughter. She had inherited the exotic beauty and tempestuous passions of her fore-bears. Although she was nearly 40 Titus fell in love with her. Their affair was to last for many years.

Accompanied by Agrippa Vespasian marched against Tiberias. The city had only half-heartedly joined the revolt and surrendered without a blow. The Romans now turned on Taricheae. The city was stormed but a large number nof the rebels tried to escape in boats. Vespasian built rafts and sent his archers after them. The rebel force, in their boats, was wiped out and their bodies left to rot in the water. Many of the townsfolk were captured. The old and weak were executed and the rest sent into slavery.

The harsh example of Taricheae paid off. All the towns and strongholds in the area surrendered. Only Gischala, Gamala and Mt. Tabor held out. Gamala was the most formidable position and Vespasian decided to knock it out first. It was built on the side of a precipitious spur jutting out from the Golan plateau into the valley of the Daliyyot. The only approach was long a narrow ridge some 100m below the level of the plateau.

The legionaries managed to breach the walls but when they broke in they were forced to fight an uphill battle in the narrow streets. They were unable to manoeuvre because their comrades were crowding in behind them. They climbed up on to the roofs of the houses which were built in terraces up the hillside. Under the weight the houses collapsed bringing down others beneath them, like dominoes. Many of the Romans fell to their deaths. Others were buried in the rubble and still more choked to death in the clouds of dust. The defenders encouraged by this 'act of God' counter-attacked, causing panic amongst the Romans who fumbled around in the blinding dust striking out at each other.

Some days later legionaries working under the cover of darkness managed to dislodge some stones from the base of the largest tower which collapsed. The following morning the Romans again entered the town. This time they systematically exterminated the population. Those who were not killed flung themselves off the citadel. Only two women survived.

During the siege Vespasian had sent a detachment to reduce the Jewish forces on Mt. Tabor. Some of the rebels were killed but the majority escaped to Jerusalem. A second expedition, headed by Vespasian's son Titus, was sent against Gischala where the Zealot, John was holding out. But John escaped with his followers and made his way to Jerusalem.

The south end of the sea of Galilee. Here the last of the Galilean rebels were cornered. They took to the water but were hunted down by Vespasian's archers mounted on rafts.

Roman siege techniques
2: battering rams

A mobile battering ram. The illustration has been cut away to show the legionaries pulling the beam back. They would then run forward with it. The tower at the back contains water to put out fires. On the top floor is a small catapult.

Battering rams

The Romans used the suspension type of ram. This consisted of a long beam suspended by a rope or chain. The beam was bound with ropes to stop it splintering and then covered with hides to protect it from fire. The head of the ram was iron-plated.

The ram could be suspended from a frame which would be enclosed in a protective housing or it could be built into a sturdy mobile housing. These housings were covered with green wicker and layers of hide padded with seaweed or wet straw as a protection against bombardment.

BELOW: the site of Gamala. The town was built on the steeply sloping hillside. The remains of the walls can still be seen. The rocky mass rising at the far end is the citadel. The last of the defenders threw themselves to their deaths from here. The town could only be approached along the route of the modern path. The sea of Galilee can be seen in the background.

RIGHT: the remains of one of the houses built on terraces up the hillside.

Massacres at Jerusalem

When John of Gischala arrived at Jerusalem he was given a hero's welcome by the Zealots. He blamed the authorities in Jerusalem for the loss of Galilee and even accused them of being in league with the Romans. A purge began and many of the leading citizens were arrested and executed without trial.

The Zealots had taken over the Temple platform. They were convinced that all the senior priests had been corrupted by the Romans and none was fit to hold the high priesthood. They selected a new high priest from among their own followers. The chief priests were outraged. Supported by the majority of the population they stormed the Temple platform.

The Zealots were driven back into the Temple itself. But the chief priests dared not attack the sanctuary without ritually purifying their followers and the Zealots used this respite to call in help from Idumaea. Twenty thousand men answered the call and marched on Jerusalem. The chief priests barred the gates against them but one dark, stormy night the Idumaeans were secretly let in. The chief priests and their supporters were slaughtered and a reign of terror began. Those suspected of Roman sympathies were massacred. Through all this, Jesus the son of Ananias uttered his forebodings – 'Woe to thee Jerusalem!'

The Christian community in Jerusalem must have recalled the prophecies of Jesus of Nazareth – 'This generation shall not pass away until all these things are accomplished.' Maybe they believed that God would intervene. Maybe they joined the revolt. Legend has it that they fled across Jordan to the non-Jewish city of Pella in Peraea.

Early in the spring of 68 AD Vespasian led his forces against the Jewish communities in Peraea. Gadora (Es Salt) the capital was betrayed but the revolutionary party managed to escape. The Romans overtook them just before they reached the village of Bethennabris. Many were cut down along the road. The rest made a dash for the village. The Romans, following up, stormed the walls, massacred the population and set the village on fire. This caused panic in the surrounding countryside where the peasants gathered together all their livestock and fled for the Jordan, hoping to escape across the river into Judea. The Jordan was swollen by the winter rains and unfordable. Unable to escape the peasants were cut down along the banks or drowned trying to cross the river.

Before the terrified population could recover the Romans struck home capturing all the towns and villages as far south as Machaerus.

Samaria had made only a token resistance which had been put down during the Galilean campaign. Only Judea and the area to the south remained in arms. Vespasian now marched south through the coastal plain, knocking out key towns on the roads leading to Jerusalem. Garrisons were installed and Jerusalem was entirely cut off from the west. The Fifth Legion dug in at Emmaus and a strong garrison was placed at Adida on the road from Joppa to Jerusalem.

Vespasian now moved through Samaria and descended on Jericho. Here the Tenth Legion dug in, cutting Jerusalem off from the east. It must have been now that the Essenes at Qumran hid their scrolls and fled.

In the autumn of 68 AD news arrived that Nero was dead and that Galba the governor of Spain had ascended the throne. Vespasian called a halt to the war and sent Titus to Rome to make his submission to the new emperor. Titus got only as far as Greece when he heard that Galba had been murdered. After 100 years a new power struggle was beginning at Rome. Titus returned to Judea to await the outcome.

A new revolution now flared up in the south. Another Messiah had appeared. He was a man of immense size and strength. This was Simon Bar-Giora. He was not a Zealot but he was governed by the same extreme nationalism and conviction as John of Gischala. He collected a large band of followers and devastated Idumaea.

Vespasian had remained inactive for almost a year. The position in Rome was still uncertain but he decided that he must act before the situation in Judea got out of hand and all his preliminary work was undone. In the early summer of 69 AD he led his army into the field again. He tightened his circuit to the north of Jerusalem capturing Gophna and cutting the roads to the north. He then invaded Idumaea. Hebron was burned and the whole area devastated. Jerusalem was now cut off. Only the fortresses of Herodium, Masada and Machaerus held out.

Meanwhile, in Jerusalem, the purges continued. In desperation the citizens turned to Simon Bar-Giora and invited him into the city. They hoped that he would oust John of Gischala who had become the leader of the Zealots. Instead they found themselves at the mercy of two fanatics. Simon launched an attack on the Temple but was unable to take it. The Zealots strengthened their fortifications by erecting four huge towers along the perimeter of the outer court. The city was divided into two hostile camps each preying on the citizenry.

Roman siege techniques 3: catapults

RIGHT: **1** reconstruction of medium-sized catapult capable of throwing stones of about 12 kilos.
2 Cut-away section of the 'springs' of a catapult. These were tightened by twisting at the top and bottom.
3 Heavy catapult stones found at Herodium.

BELOW: the Judean campaign. In the late winter of 68 AD Vespasian invaded Peraea. He took Gadora and left the Tenth Legion to complete the conquest of the area. In the spring he marched through the coastal plain cutting the roads leading up to Jerusalem. He left the Fifth Legion at Emmaus, crossed over to the Jordan valley and established the Tenth Legion at Jericho. The following year he completed the blockade of Jerusalem by capturing Gophna and Hebron.

Catapults

There were two types of catapult, arrow-shooters and stone-throwers. Both were like oversize cross-bows powered by 'springs' of twisted hair or sinew. The strength of these 'springs' was so great that the bow string had to be winched back. The size of these machines varied from small sharp-shooters (scorpions) about 2m long to vast engines capable of throwing a stone weighing 50 kilos.

The central part of the machine, the slider **A** was pulled back along the stock **B** bringing the bowstring with it. The bowstring was released by a trigger mechanism **C**.

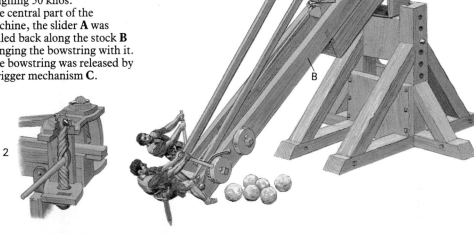

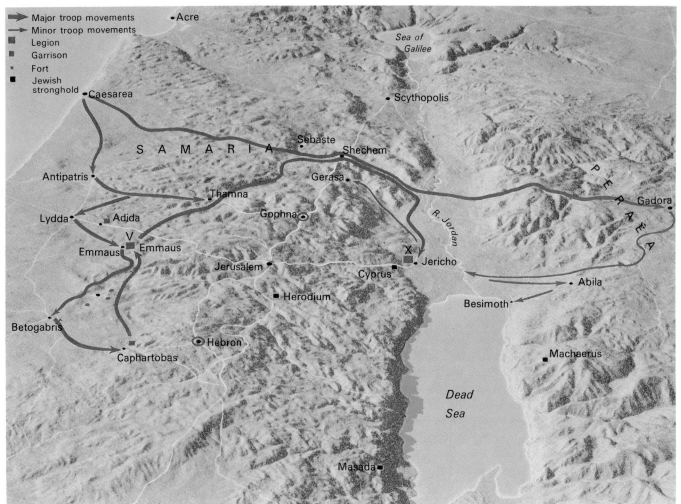

Vespasian enters the lists

Italy was in chaos. Otho had ascended the throne only to find that Vitellius the governor of Germany had also been declared emperor by his troops. Otho marched northwards to meet the threat but was defeated by the German legions. The empire had now become the prize of the strongest and Vespasian entered the fray.

On July 1st he was proclaimed emperor in Egypt and almost simultaneously the legions in Judea and Syria declared their support. When Josephus had been captured he had tried to ingratiate himself with Vespasian by prophesying that he would one day become emperor. This prophesy was now judged to be divinely inspired and Josephus was given his freedom.

By the middle of July all the eastern provinces had declared their support for Vespasian. Mucianus, the governor of Syria, was sent on the long march to Italy whilst Vespasian withdrew to Alexandria, the nearest point of contact with Rome. Before Mucianus could reach Italy the war had been decided.

Part of the Danubian army had been told to occupy the route into north-eastern Italy and hold it open for Mucianus. Their commander had exceeded his orders and advanced into the Po Valley. He was cut off and forced to fight a battle near Cremona. All through the night the battle raged. At dawn the eastern legions raised a shout in praise of the sun. This was their custom but the other side believed that Mucianus had arrived. They broke ranks and fled.

When Vespasian was informed of his victory he handed over the conduct of the Jewish war to Titus and sailed for Rome.

Titus was given another legion, the Twelfth called Fulminata, from Syria. He moved on Jerusalem from the north picking up the Fifth Legion from Emmaus en route. He occupied Mt. Scopus, about 1½km north-east of the city. Here he established two camps. Soon after the Tenth Legion arrived coming up from Jericho and pitched camp on the Mount of Olives.

During the winter the Zealots had split into two hostile factions. Eleazar, who had been leader of the party before John took over, occupied the inner court of the Temple with his followers. John was caught between Eleazar and Simon Bar-Giora in the city. The conflict developed into a war of attrition with each party trying to destroy the other by burning its food supply. Warehouses were burned and the corn which had been gathered in case of a siege were destroyed.

RIGHT: A model of Jerusalem showing the aqueducts and cisterns which supplied the city with water. This shows the only remains that have been found and some of these are of uncertain date. Most houses also had cisterns for the collection of rain water.

Lower Aqueduct

Upper City

Lower City

Temple

LEFT: the remains of the triple gate built by Agrippa I beneath the Damascus Gate at Jerusalem. This shows one of the small side entrances used by pedestrians. There would have been a much larger arch to the right of this and another small one beyond it.

BELOW: an aerial photograph of Jerusalem from the east. The Kedron valley and the remains of the temple platform are in the foreground. The upper city is behind it.

Jerusalem after Herod

There had been little monumental building since the time of Herod the Great, but Jerusalem had increased greatly in size. The suburbs now spread far to the north of Herod's city. Agrippa had tried to enclose these within the city walls.

The aqueducts

Jerusalem had insufficient water for a large population. The city was built on top of the central ridge. (The Temple platform has an elevation of 735m and the citadel 765m.) Any water flowing into the city had to come from a higher level than this as aqueducts rely on gravity.

The remains of several aqueducts have been found south of Jerusalem. Two of these, the 'Upper' and the 'Lower' aqueducts, run from Solomon's Pools about 3½km south west of Bethlehem. They supply water to the citadel and the Temple. The higher of Solomon's pools has an altitude of 790m.

The famous aqueduct of Pontius Pilate probably ran from the Wadi Arrub to Solomon's Pools. It is very long and follows the sinuous contours of the wadi to keep a correct height.

The siege begins

Having secured his position on Mt. Scopus, Titus began to level off the area between his camp and the city walls. Every fence, wall, monument and tree was flattened. Even the caves and gullies were filled up. Once the area was cleared the Romans moved in closer and established two new camps – one at the north-west corner of the city and the other opposite the citadel. These were about 400m from the wall, just out of catapult range. The Tenth Legion remained on the Mount of Olives.

Besides the citizens there were rather more than 20,000 troops in the city. Simon had about 10,000 followers plus 5,000 remaining Idumaeans (most of the Idumaeans had returned home). These took over the northern and western defences. John and Eleazar eventually buried their differences. They had about 8,400 Zealots and held the eastern defences.

Titus launched his first assault just north of the citadel. Whilst three legions began throwing up a ramp here, the Tenth kept the Zealots busy by bombarding the Temple from the slopes of the Mount of Olives. The huge stones thrown by the larger catapults caused devastation on the Temple platform. The Zealots soon realised that they could see the missiles coming as they were light coloured and stood out against the dark hillside in the background. When

a stone was launched, a lookout would shout a warning and all those in line of fire would throw themselves to the ground. The Romans soon caught on and darkened the stones. Jesus the son of Ananias was still continuing his mournful dirge – 'Woe to thee Jerusalem!' – after nearly seven and a half years, when he was struck by one of these catapult stones and killed.

Once the ramp was completed the battering rams were brought up. The artillery moved in closer to give covering fire and the pounding began. As the ram struck the wall a great cry was raised within the city. By ancient law, surrender had to be unconditional after the battering ram struck the first blow.

For the first time the defenders acted together. They lined the ramparts and hurled firebrands at the infernal machines. But still the pounding continued. They dashed through the gates and threw themselves on the Romans. Again and again they were driven back and the pounding went on.

The Romans now moved up huge iron-clad towers from which they could sweep the defenders from the battlements with their archers and light artillery. On the 15th day of the siege the largest of the battering rams, which the Jews had nick-named Victor, shook down part of the wall. They abandoned the northern suburbs and withdrew to the second line of walls.

LEFT: a model of ancient Jerusalem showing the possible positions of the three northern walls. The archaeological remains are shown in black. The probable line of the outer defences is shown in brown. The Turkish wall which still remains today is shown in red. **A–A** The wall to the north of the old city. This had towers about 12m wide but the wall has no proper foundations.
B The Damascus Gate. The remains beneath this are undoubtedly from the mid first century AD.
C–C This part of the Turkish wall is very weak and is defended only by a ditch. It would have presented no obstacle to the Romans. The dotted brown line **D–D** shows a stronger line of defence.
E–E–E Possible line of the second wall.
F–F–F Probable line of the first north wall.
G The Hippicus Tower.
H The Antonia Fortress.
J The Psephinus Tower(?)

An archaeological problem

Josephus gives us a detailed description of the walls of Jerusalem. Unfortunately the archaeological evidence does not fit his description.

The description of Josephus

Josephus tells us that where the city was protected by deep valleys it was defended by a single wall. This refers to the whole of the southern half of the city, i.e. south of the citadel and the Temple. This presents no problems and the line of most of this wall has been discovered. He calls this the first or old wall. To the north of the city where there were no natural defences Josephus claims that there were three walls. This is where the problems start.

The first north wall

The first of the northern walls ran from the Hippicus tower at the northern end of the citadel, past the market place (Xystus) to the Temple portico. This would appear to join up with the viaduct leading from the Temple to the upper city and again presents no real problem.

The second north wall

The second of the northern walls began at the Gennath Gate and joined up with the Antonia Fortress. Since the site of the Gennath Gate is unknown, and because this area abounds with bits of wall, there is no way that the course of the wall can be worked out. A possible course is shown in white in the illustration on the left.

The third north wall

The third wall began at the Hippicus Tower. It stretched north to the Psephinus Tower and descended opposite the tomb of queen Helena of Adiabene. It then bent round a corner tower and joined the old wall at the Kedron valley. This description fits a long stretch of wall discovered north of the old city. But there is one complication. Josephus tells us that the third wall was begun by Agrippa I and completed by the Zealots. A gate from Agrippa's wall has been discovered beneath the Damascus Gate nearly 500m south of this wall (see page 82).
Some scholars think that the northern-most wall was only an advanced defence but this is not very satisfactory.

ABOVE: model of Jerusalem seen from the north to illustrate the Roman siege of the city.
A–A The first main camp of Titus.
B Titus' second main camp.
C–C Titus' third main camp within the walls of the city.
D–D The second camp of the Fifth Legion. The first camp of the Fifth Legion was behind Titus' first camp (off the picture at the bottom).
E–E The camp of the Tenth Legion.
The broken red line shows the line of the Roman siege wall.
F The Damascus Gate.
G The Hippicus tower.
H The Antonia Fortress.
J The tomb of queen Helena of Adiabene.
The arrows and numbers show the successive Roman attacks.

Famine sets in

Titus now moved his camp into the town occupying the whole northern sector. The rams were moved up against the second wall and in five days this also was breached. The Romans burst through the narrow opening but the Jews rallied and drove them out again. Four days later the Romans launched a second attack. This time they captured the wall and demolished it. The north end of the Temple platform and the Antonia fortress were completely exposed.

In the city food stocks were beginning to dwindle. The Romans were aware of this and slowed down their operations. Their pay was due and a pay parade was held in dress uniform in full view of the defenders, in order to impress upon them the sheer futility of their resistance.

It took four days to pay the four legions. When it was over and still the Jews remained defiant, the siege began again in earnest. Titus split his forces. The Twelfth and the Fifth Legions began to throw up a ramp against the Antonia whilst the Tenth and Fifteenth began a similar ramp against the walls of the citadel. Josephus was now made to pay the price of his freedom. He was sent round the walls to make propaganda speeches trying to undermine the morale of the defenders. Though some of the ordinary citizens did desert, the Zealots poured abuse on him. They had no doubt that, in the end, God would intervene and the Messiah would lead them to victory.

As the famine began to set in, fights broke out in the city over the remaining supplies. Those who had come into the city – the followers of John and Simon – had no source of food after the public supplies had gone. So an even more terrible split developed between the revolutionaries and the citizens. The houses of the wealthy were broken into and searched. Their occupants were often tortured and killed in the frantic quest for food.

As the siege now entered its final stages the Romans unleashed a campaign of terror hoping to frighten the Jews into surrender. The famine was driving the poorer citizens out of the city at night in search of food. If captured they were scourged and crucified in front of the walls. Sometimes hundreds each day met this grisly fate. The Romans broke the monotony by nailing their victims up in different poses.

The erection of the ramp in front of the Antonia took seventeen days. But John and his Zealots on the Temple platform had been cutting a tunnel beneath the ramp, propping it up with timbers as they went. When it was completed they set fire to the props.

The siege of the Antonia

There was a rumble like thunder and the timber walls of the ramp collapsed into the mine. At first the Romans saw only a great cloud of dust but as this settled flames broke through, setting fire to the timber. They could only stand aghast as seventeen days labour was consumed.

The ramp against the citadel suffered a similar fate. Here the rams had already begun to pound the wall. Simon's men formed a suicide squad which burst from the city and set fire to the screens surrounding the machines. In the face of certain death the Jewish squad stood their ground and struggled with the Romans to stop them pulling away the rams. The fire spread to the ramp itself and the whole structure was destroyed.

Titus had hoped for a quick end to the siege. He now realised that he would have to revert to the more arduous methods at which the Romans excelled. A Roman's greatest assets were his refusal to accept defeat and his willingness to work like a slave. His motto might well have been 'Dig for victory'. Within three days a rough wall nearly 8km in length had been erected around the city following the line of the hilltops to the east, south and west. This was joined to the main camp in the northern part of the city and linked it with the camps on the Mount of Olives and opposite the citadel. Thirteen forts were placed along it. These were garrisoned by auxiliary troops. This wall cut the city off from the outside world. There was no longer any hope of escape or relief.

As the famine grew worse so the desertions increased. Many of the deserters swallowed their money so that it would not be confiscated by the Romans. When one of these was caught retrieving his money the soldiers went berserk. Rumour spread that the deserters were full of gold and many were ripped open and their bowels searched.

The legions now concentrated their efforts against the Antonia and began to rebuild the ramp. The whole countryside had been stripped of trees to build the original ramps. New timber had to be brought in from a distance of 18km.

The new ramp was completed in three weeks. John and his Zealots tried to fire it but they were driven off. The rams were moved up and the pounding began again. A group of legionaries forming a 'tortoise' with their shields managed to get up to the walls and dislodge four stones. The wall refused to topple. But the ram had done its work. That night the mine which John had dug to destroy the original ramp caved in and the wall collapsed with it.

The Antonia fortress

Building the Antonia
The Antonia or Bira fortress had been built originally by the Hasmonaean kings at the weakest point in the defences of Jerusalem. Here the Bethesda Hill sloped down to the walls making them very vulnerable. There was a small knoll on this slope. The sides of this were cut away to form a sheer cliff face on the exposed sides. A fortified catapult battery was built on top to cover the approaches to the walls. In front of it was a wide ditch and a low wall which kept the attackers back from the main building but under constant fire from the catapults. This was the normal Greek concept of defence.

Herod's fortress
Herod refashioned the fortress giving it luxurious apartments and turning it into a small palace. When he enlarged the Temple he incorporated the fortress into the Temple complex. From this time the fortress acquired a new and sinister purpose – to keep a check on the activities of the Temple. He built a high tower at the south-east corner of the fortress from which everything in the area could be seen.

Josephus' description
Josephus tells us that the Antonia was built on a rock 50 cubits (c25m) high. The face of the rock was covered with smooth flagstones. The fortress was 40 cubits (c20m) high with a tower at each of its four corners. Three were 50 cubits (c25m) high. The one overlooking the temple was 70 cubits (c35m) high.

Archaeological evidence
Only the rock on which the Antonia stood remains. This has a maximum height of 11m – less than half Josephus' figure. The fortress could have had a solid stone base raising it to the required height.
The rock is 'L'-shaped making it difficult to envisage four corner towers. It has been suggested that the 'L'-shaped cutting was made at a later time but this seems unlikely as it lines up with the Temple porticoes. The tower overlooking the Temple may have been an afterthought and built on a solid stone base.
Traces of the fronting ditch have been found. There is also a cistern (Struthion Pool) opposite the north-west corner of the rock. This must have been part of the defences.

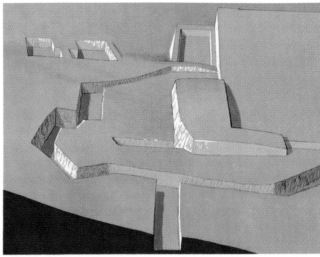

TOP: the rock cutting at the north-west corner of the Temple platform. This is the only visible trace of the Antonia.

ABOVE: the rock cuttings and ancient structures at the north end of the Temple platform. The ditches are mainly hypothetical.

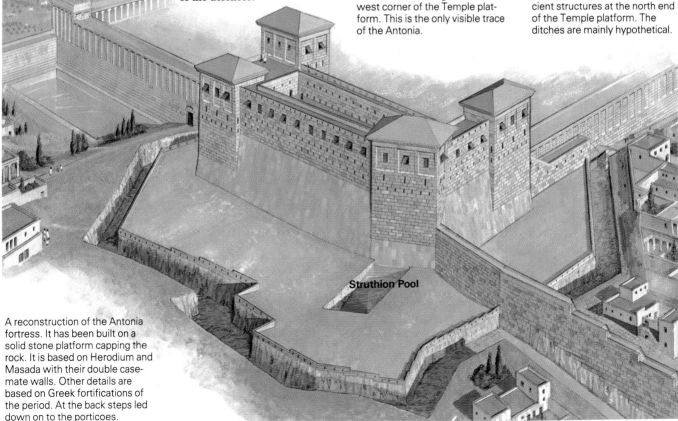

Struthion Pool

A reconstruction of the Antonia fortress. It has been built on a solid stone platform capping the rock. It is based on Herodium and Masada with their double casemate walls. Other details are based on Greek fortifications of the period. At the back steps led down on to the porticoes.

The assault on the Temple

The Antonia falls

John had foreseen the collapse of the Antonia wall and had built another wall inside. The spirits of the legionaries sunk when they saw it. Whilst it was possible to get at it by clambering over the rubble, to try to storm it would be suicidal as only a few could get through at a time.

Three nights later a group of auxiliaries with a trumpeter silently scaled the wall before dawn and overpowered the guards. They then sounded the trumpet to call in the rest of the Romans. The Jews, believing that the fortress was already captured, panicked and retreated to the Temple platform. The Romans following up burst through into the outer court. Here they met a fanatical defence by the Zealots and were driven back on the Antonia. However, they managed to establish a forward post at the north-east corner of the Temple platform and kept it supplied and reinforced through the tunnel that John had dug under the Antonia to collapse the original ramp. On the day that the Romans set foot on the Temple platform the daily sacrifice in the Temple ceased.

The Romans tried another night attack but the Zealots were not to be caught off guard twice. A fierce battle was fought but only a limited number of Roman soldiers could be brought into action and they were driven back again. Meanwhile the Romans began to demolish the Antonia, overthrowing even its foundations, so that the ramp could be extended right through the fortress and form a broad approach road.

The Zealots now set fire to the north-west porticoes to cut off the Antonia from the Temple courts. As the Jews continued to use the undamaged portions to launch missile attacks the Romans set fire to them and destroyed even more of the porticoes. A few days later, having stuffed the rafters with inflammable material the Jews abandoned the western portico. The Romans saw it was unguarded, dashed forward and climbed up on to it. When the roof was crowded with soldiers the Zealots set fire to it. Many of the blazing soldiers leapt to their deaths. Few survived.

The Romans now tried to force the north gate of the Temple platform. They set fire to the northern portico so that those defending the gate would have no cover. Two more ramps had been erected on the western side of the Temple platform. The timber for these had to be dragged in from a vast distance. The rams were brought into play again but their pounding proved useless against the colossal Herodian masonry.

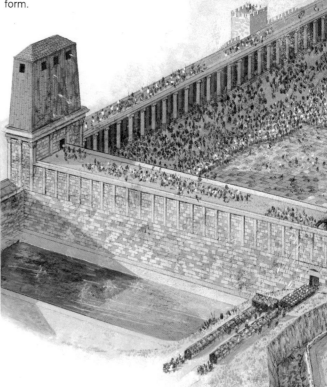

The Antonia fortress has been destroyed leaving the highest tower as an observation post. It may have been flat-topped as shown here. The rubble from the fortress was used to extend the ramp through to the Temple platform.

The Antonia ramp
The Temple could only really be attacked down the Bethesda Hill against its north-west corner where the Antonia fortress stood. Anywhere else the approach was uphill and blocked by the massive containing walls of the Temple platform. The Romans erected their ramp over the Struthion Pool filling the dip between the Bethesda Hill and the Antonia. It formed a level causeway along which the Romans could bring up their siege engines and attack the fortress walls above the level of its foundations. This ramp was only the right half of what is shown in the picture. It was later widened with the rubble from the fortress. Josephus causes some confusion as he talks of pairs of ramps. He is probably referring to the two containing walls which were made of timber.

Razing the Antonia
Having captured the Antonia the Romans found themselves suspended some 25m above the Temple platform. Their only access was down the steps on to the porticoes and from there down on to the platform itself. Only small numbers of troops could be sent down this way. By destroying the fortress right down to the rock Titus was able to extend his ramp through to the Temple platform. He was now able to bring up large bodies of troops.

The destruction of the Temple

Once the ramp through the remains of the Antonia was complete the Romans were able to bring large bodies of troops and even cavalry down on to the Temple platform. The Zealots were no match for the Romans in hand-to-hand combat and were relentlessly driven back into the Temple itself.

Titus had concluded that there coud be no peace as long as the Temple remained. Josephus' claim that he tried to save it was wishful thinking. Titus gave orders for the gates to the inner courts and the nearby porticoes to be set on fire. The fires blazed throughout the night. The following day they were extinguished, the area around the inner courts cleared of debris, and the Romans prepared for the final assault.

The next morning they moved in for the kill. The Zealots burst from the inner courts and threw themselves on the Romans. But their fate was sealed. Titus now sent in the cavalry. The result was devastating. Seeing their comrades cut down, the Zealots fled to the inner courts. The Romans burst in after them driving them back into the sanctuary itself. One soldier with the help of his comrades climbed up the outside of the Temple and threw a piece of burning wood through a window into one of the side rooms. More fire brands followed and in no time the outer rooms were ablaze.

A route was cleared so that Titus and his generals could go into the sanctuary. But they found it empty. The sacred furniture had all been removed by the priests. The building was abandoned to the flames and ancient Judaism ceased to exist.

Later, one of the priests offered to hand over some of the Temple treasure and the high priest's vestments in return for his life, but the bulk of the treasure was never found.

On the 14th March 1952 a copper scroll was discovered in the caves at Qumran. It was very corroded. At first it seemed impossible to unroll. Finally it was very carefully cut into strips at Manchester University and translated. It appears to list the hiding places of the Temple treasure. Many scholars have dismissed it as a hoax. Others passionately defend its authenticity. What is certain is that although it may have been possible to identify these locations in ancient times it is impossible today.

The wretched, starving and half crazed survivors had taken refuge on the roof of the basilica. In revenge for what had been done to their comrades on the western portico, the Romans set the building on fire.

Even to the end the defenders had believed that God would intervene.

The abomination and the desolation

The Romans now carried their standards into the Temple and sacrificed before them. It was the traditional Roman sacrifice of an ox, a sheep and a pig – the final abomination.

John had escaped from the Temple but he was utterly disillusioned. Accompanied by Simon he tried to come to terms with Titus. They offered to withdraw to the desert with their followers. The Roman refused to grant any terms. It had to be unconditional surrender.

The old city was now at Titus' mercy. He handed it over to the soldiers' pleasure and then burned it. The remaining defenders fled to the upper city and the legions were now forced to besiege this too. The approaches on the east were too steep for an assault and on the west side were the massive defences of the citadel. More ramps were needed – more timber would have to be found. The four legions set to work raising a ramp against the citadel whilst the auxiliaries prepared for an uphill assault on the east. Titus had refused to grant terms for surrender, but faced with the alternative of starvation many Jews deserted. Most of these were sold into slavery.

In eighteen days the ramps were completed. When the Romans broke in they met no opposition. Famine and disillusion had done their work for them. They slaughtered everyone they found. As the sun set the massacre ceased and the city was given up to the flames. The siege had lasted five months.

Masses of prisoners were rounded up. The old and the ill were killed off and the remainder confined in the court of the women on the Temple platform. All the Zealots and their supporters were separated and executed. The 700 tallest and most handsome of the prisoners were reserved for the triumph. The rest were sent to the amphitheatres of the east where during the autumn of 70 AD they were killed for sport. Some were killed in combats, some by wild beasts and others were burned alive.

Jerusalem was now systematically destroyed. The walls flattened. The Temple and its platform were broken up. Only the three massive towers, Phasael, Hippicus and Miriam which had been built by Herod at the north end of the citadel were left standing. These together with a portion of the west wall, were to form the defences of the camp of the Tenth Legion, called Fretensis, which was to remain in Judea.

When the upper city fell many of the defenders escaped into the tunnels beneath the city. Ultimately they were forced to surface and were captured. Among these were Simon and John. They were both sent to Italy to take part in the triumph.

Evidence of the destruction

RIGHT: the excavations to the south-east of the Temple platform. The containing wall can be seen on the right side with the massive Herodian masonry at the bottom. The monumental stairway in the centre has been restored by the excavators.

BELOW: the kitchen of the Burnt House in the old Jewish quarter of Jerusalem showing the skeletal forearm as it was found. (After N. Avigad.)

RIGHT: fragments of columns found to the south of the Temple platform.

Burnt houses

Much excavation has taken place at Jerusalem since 1967 when the old city was captured by the Israelis. The whole area around the southern end of the Temple platform has been uncovered and numerous 'digs' have taken place in the old Jewish quarter and the upper city.

Wherever there have been excavations evidence of the Roman destruction has come to light. Weapons, both Jewish and Roman, have been found and many of the houses beneath the Jewish quarter show signs of burning.

Early in the excavations a burnt house was discovered. In its kitchen a skeletal forearm was found – mute testimony of violent death.

The destruction of the Temple

No excavation has taken place in the vicinity of the Temple as it is now an Islamic holy place. But to the south of the Temple platform the excavations have revealed a great deal.

The ruins of the meeting hall seem to have been thrown over the southern edge of the platform. Remains of columns were found strewn across the area. Much of the containing wall of the platform was also demolished. This can be clearly seen for there is a clear division between the massive Herodian masonry and the later smaller stonework.

Josephus gives no details of the storming of the Old City. It is possible that the Romans levelled the area before the assault.

The siege of Masada

The end of Judea

In Rome Vespasian and Titus celebrated a triumph over the Jews. The Temple treasure and the prisoners were paraded around the city. Simon was whipped through the streets with a halter around his neck before being ceremonially strangled. John was imprisoned for life.

A new governor was sent out to reduce the final strongholds of Herodium, Machaerus and Masada but he died before the work was completed. It was left to his successor Flavius Silva to reduce Masada which was held by the Sicarii. He subdued the surrounding country and then moved in on the fortress.

Silva had the Tenth Legion and six auxiliary cohorts with him. He encamped one half of the legion on the low ground to the east and the other half on the higher ground to the west of the fortress. Here he established his headquarters. The auxiliary cohorts were placed in six separate camps. A siege wall was thrown up around the base of the rock to prevent anybody escaping.

The defenders had almost unlimited supplies of food and water but the Romans had to have everything brought in from a distance. Masada could not be starved out. It had to be stormed. The cliffs could never be scaled in force and Silva was compelled to undertake the incredible task of throwing up a ramp. It took seven months.

When the ramp was complete an iron-clad tower and battering ram were winched up to a stone platform at the top. The wall collapsed under the pounding but the Sicarii had backed it up with earth and timber. The Romans were unable to breach it and finally set it on fire. The following morning they broke in. Not a sound met their ears. During the night the whole garrison, after killing their wives and children, had killed themselves. Only two old women and five children survived to tell the tale. Masada has now become an Israeli shrine where the army swears the oath of allegiance.

The 960 suicides at Masada brought the war to an end. Incredible though it may seem, 60 years later the Jews tried again. Another leader, Simon bar Kokhba led a revolt which was provoked by plans to build a temple to Jupiter on the Temple Mount. It was a guerrilla war with all the atrocities that that entailed. The country was devastated. Nearly 1,000 villages were destroyed. When the revolt had been crushed Jerusalem was rebuilt and renamed Aelia Capitolina. Jews were forbidden to enter it on pain of death.

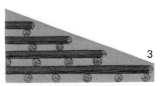

LEFT: **1** schematic plan of the ramp showing its original shape. **A** The stone platform at the top. **2** Section of the ramp at **B–B**. **3** Schematic drawing of the bottom of the ramp showing how the timbers were probably laid.

BELOW: aerial view of Masada from the north showing:
F Main Roman camp and Silva's headquarters. Cohorts 1 to 5 of the Tenth Legion were probably billeted here.
B The camp of the other five legionary cohorts.
A, C, D, E, G and **H**. The camps of the six auxiliary cohorts.
J The ramp.
The siege wall and interval towers can be clearly seen linking all the auxiliary camps except **C**.

The Roman siege lines

The site of Masada is unique. The whole of the Roman siege can be traced on the ground even though the area has never been excavated. All the camps are there – so are siege lines and the remains of the ramp.

A winter siege

The siege took place in the winter of 72/73 AD. The first thing that the Romans would have done would be to divert the aqueducts for their own use. This water supply was seasonal (autumn and spring). Further supplies had to be brought up from En Gedi. Jewish prisoners were used for this.

The ramp

The ramp was built by the legionaries and is a tribute to their engineering skill and perseverance. It had an incline of twenty degrees. This must have presented considerable problems for the Roman engineers who were more used to filling valleys with their ramps than climbing mountains with them. Pieces of the timber containing walls can still be seen sticking out of the ramp.

ABOVE: the building of the ramp. It was built by the legionaries who wear body armour and side arms. They were protected by screens and sheds. Materials were brought up through covered passageways.

BELOW: the remains of the ramp at Masada.

When were the gospels written?

A hundred years ago it was generally believed that the gospels were written soon after the death of Jesus. But this view has since been questioned mainly because of the prophecy describing the destruction of the Temple.

Mark's gospel is generally accepted as the earliest. He gives a very brief version of the prophecy referring only to the throwing down of the stones. In Matthew and Luke this is more developed and they describe the city 'fenced' in by the enemy. This has led most scholars to place the writing of Matthew and Luke after the siege of Jerusalem in 70 AD.

Mark and the Zealots

Some scholars have noted that when listing the apostles Mark refers to Simon as the 'kananaios'. The gospel was written in Greek but this is not a Greek word. Mark offers no explanation although he has just explained that 'boanerges' meant 'Sons of thunder'. The word 'kananaios' was Aramaic for Zealot.

Mark was writing for a Roman audience and he clearly felt that it was unwise to translate this provocative word and involve Jesus with the Zealots. This suggests that the gospel was written at a time when the name Zealot was well known and despised at Rome – in other words during the Jewish War.

Dates and authors

It seems likely that Mark's gospel was written between 66 and 70 AD. Matthew and Luke must be placed after 70 and before 100 AD. John's gospel is generally accepted as the last. It was probably written right at the end of the century. Matthew clearly uses Mark as a source of information (or they had a common source). Therefore it is highly unlikely that he was a witness to the events he describes. It seems equally unlikely that a gospel written as late as John's could have been by an apostle.

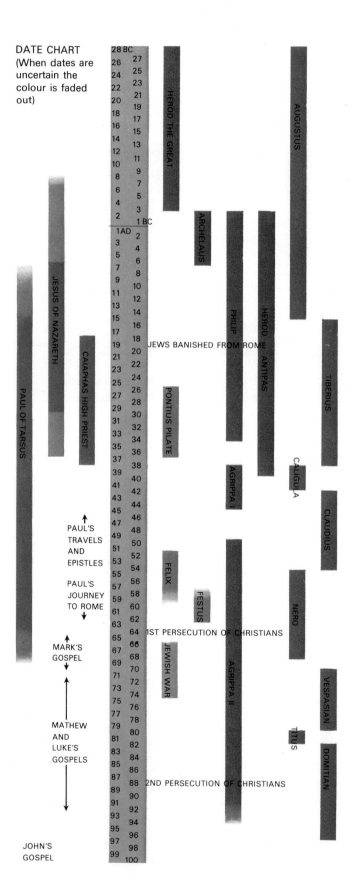

DATE CHART
(When dates are uncertain the colour is faded out)

When was Jesus born?

Most scholars place the birth of Jesus about 7 BC. This is because Herod the Great died in 4 BC and Matthew tells how Herod tried to kill Jesus as a baby. However Luke seems to tell an entirely different story. If you believe in the literal truth of the New Testament the two accounts have to be made to interlock.

Luke's account

Luke's account is very detailed but he does not mention the massacre of the little children. He connects the birth of John the Baptist with Herod the Great (1.5) and says that Jesus was six months younger than John. (1.26). So far his account presents no problems. But he goes on to relate the story of the Roman census conducted by Quirinius the governor of Syria and how Mary and Joseph had to go to Bethlehem to register (2.1–5). This census was held in 6/7 AD when Judea was made a Roman province.

Historians have rejected the idea that there might have been another census run by a man with the same name about 13 years earlier.

The crucifixion

The date of the crucifixion is equally elusive – 30 AD is the most popular date. Matthew and Mark tell us that Caiaphas was high priest (c18–37 AD), Pilate was governor (26–36 AD) and Antipas was tetrarch of Galilee (4 BC–36 AD).

John has the Jews say to Jesus at the beginning of his ministry 'this Temple took 46 years to build . . .' (2.20). The Temple was begun in 20 BC so this must have been said after 26 AD. Luke tells us that John the Baptist began preaching in the 15th year of the reign of Tiberius (3.1–2). This should be 28–29 AD. Jesus must have started his ministry at least two or three years later. Luke adds that he was about 30 (3.23). If Jesus was born in 7 BC he would be nearly 40. If we accept Luke's birth date of 6 AD he would be 26 or 27. Is it possible that Luke's birth date is right?

Glossary

Acre: (modern Akko, ancient Ptolemais) – the most southerly port of Syria. Whenever there was trouble in Palestine the governor of Syria would move troops down here.

Agrippa I: Grandson of Herod the Great – made king of the area to the north and east of the Sea of Galilee by the emperor Caligula in AD37. Later he received Galilee also and in AD41 the emperor Claudius gave him the whole of Herod the Great's realm. He died in AD44.

Agrippa II: Son of Agrippa I – ruled the area to the north and east of the Sea of Galilee from AD50. He died before AD92/93.

Alexander the Great: The Macedonian (northern Greek) king who conquered a vast empire stretching from Greece to India including Palestine and Egypt.

Alexander Jannaeus: Hasmonaean king died 76BC. The most brutal of the Hasmonaean kings. The Jewish kingdom reached its greatest extent during his reign.

Antipas: Son of Herod the Great who became tetrarch of Galilee when his father died in 4BC. was removed by the emperor Caligula in AD39.

Antonia: *see* Bira fortress.

Archelaus: Son of Herod the Great – became ruler of Judea after the death of Herod in 4BC but was removed by the emperor Augustus in AD6.

Aristobulus: Brother of Miriam I, became High Priest against Herod the Great's wishes and was murdered by him soon after.

Asia Minor: Roughly equivalent to western Turkey.

Assyria: Great middle eastern empire from c 1000 to 612BC.

Babylon: capital of the Babylonian empire. The Jews were forcibly removed from Judea to Babylon (the Babylonian exile) for about 50 years during the 6th century BC.

Bedouin: A nomadic Arab.

Bira fortress: (called Baris by Josephus) The fortress just north of the Temple at Jerusalem. It was remodelled by Herod and renamed the Antonia after his patron Mark Antony.

Caesarea: Great port built by Herod the Great and named in honour of the Roman emperor Augustus who had adopted the name of his uncle Julius Caesar.

Caiaphas: High Priest from 18 to AD37.

The Capitol: The old citadel of Rome where the main temple to Jupiter the Father of the Gods was situated.

Crassus: The richest man in Rome – formed an alliance with Pompey and Julius Caesar to control Rome – defeated and killed by the Parthians in 53BC.

Essenes: An extreme sect of the Pharisees (see p. 31).

Feast of Tabernacles: One of the main Jewish feasts – was celebrated in the autumn.

Mt. Gerizim: The sacred mountain of the Samaritans where they built their own temple. It rises just south of Shechem (see map on page 15).

Gessius Florus: The last procurator of Judea. His harsh rule was the 'final straw' that caused the Jews to revolt in AD66.

Hasmonaeans: The dynasty of Jewish kings founded by the Maccabean family.

Herod Philip: Son of Herod the Great and Miriam II – the first husband of Herodias.

Hyrcania: Fortress in the Judean desert notorious for its secret killings.

James, the brother of Jesus: The leader of the Christian community in Jerusalem – he was a close relative of Jesus of Nazareth.

John of Gischala: Leader of the Zealots during the Jewish revolt. He was captured when Jerusalem fell in AD70 and died in prison at Rome.

Josephus: Leader of the Jewish forces in Galilee at the beginning of the Jewish revolt AD67. He later wrote a history of the war and a history of the Jewish people (The Antiquities) which are the main source of our knowledge of this period.

Judas the Galilean: The founder of the Zealot movement. He and the Pharisee Zadduk led the resistance to the Roman census of AD6/7.

Judea: District of Palestine around Jerusalem. In its wider sense it could mean the whole of Palestine. (see map p. 11).

Julius Caesar: Roman politician and general. He gained complete control of the Roman world when he defeated Pompey in 48BC. He was assassinated in 44BC.

Maccabean brothers: The famous Jewish family that led the revolt against Antiochus IV of Syria and founded the Hasmonaean dynasty of Jewish kings.

Octavian: Nephew of Julius Caesar who later became the first Roman emperor with the title Augustus. He ruled the whole Roman Empire from 31BC to AD14.

Parthian Empire: Great eastern Empire stretching from the borders of India to Mesopotamia. Great threat to Rome in the 1st century BC.

Persian Empire: The empire conquered by Alexander. It stretched from Turkey/Egypt to India. It was founded when the Babylonian Empire fell in 538BC.

Pharisees: One of the two main sects of Judaism (see p. 30).

Philip: Son of Herod the Great. Became tetrarch of the area to the north and east of the Sea of Galilee after Herod's death in 4BC. Died in AD34.

Qumran: Site of an Essene community discovered in 1947. The Dead Sea scrolls were found here.

Sadducees: One of the two main sects of Judaism (see p. 30).

The Sanhedrin: The supreme council of the Jews. From the time of Herod its power was restricted to religious matters.

Simon Bar-Giora: Leader of the Idumaeans at the siege of Jerusalem. He was captured when the city fell and executed after the triumph of Titus at Rome.

Solomon: The most powerful and splendid of the early Jewish kings. He ruled in the mid-tenth century BC and built the original temple at Jerusalem.

Syllaeus: Prime Minister of the Nabataean Arabs and arch enemy of Herod the Great.

Syria: One of the kingdoms formed after the death of Alexander the Great in 323BC. It was conquered by the Roman general Pompey the Great and became a Roman province 64/63BC.

Tetrarch: Literally governor of a quarter – governor of a small area such as Galilee.

Zaddok: The first high priest under Solomon.

Zadduk the Pharisee: Co-founder of the Zealot movement with Judas the Galilean.

Zerubbabel: Rebuilt the Temple of Jerusalem after the return from exile in Babylon at the end of the 6th century BC.

Index